# THE
# MIRACLE
# MONTH

# THE
# MIRACLE
# MONTH

## 2ND EDITION

*30 Days to a Revolution
in Your Life*

# MITCH HOROWITZ

author of *The Miracle Club*

Published 2022 by Gildan Media LLC
aka G&D Media
www.GandDmedia.com

*The Miracle Month* copyright © 2021, *The Miracle Month Reading Group Guide* copyright © 2022, Mitch Horowitz.

Front cover design by Tom Mckeveny
Back cover author photo by Ebru Yildiz

Interior design by Meghan Day Healey of Story Horse, LLC.

Library of Congress Cataloging-in-Publication Data is available upon request

ISBN: 978-1-7225-0582-0

10   9   8   7   6   5   4   3   2

*To Toby*

# CONTENTS

INTRODUCTION
"HOW SICK?" 1

DAY 1
YOUR DAILY UNIFORM 11

DAY 2
GIVE IN 17

DAY 3
APOLOGIZE AND MEAN IT 23

DAY 4
BIKE EVERYWHERE POSSIBLE 31

DAY 5
FACE YOUR ANGER 37

DAY 6
STAND FOR SOMETHING 43

DAY 7
KEEP YOUR WORD 51

DAY 8
WHAT DO YOU WANT? 57

DAY 9
UNDERSTAND POWER 65

DAY 10
MAKE THE ASK 75

DAY 11
F COLLEGE 79

DAY 12
FIND THE SCISSORS YOURSELF 85

DAY 13
GIVE UP ONE THING THAT
CAUSES YOU PAIN 89

DAY 14
ACKNOWLEDGE THAT YOU
DO NOT KNOW 97

DAY 15
RECONSIDER FORGIVENESS 103

DAY 16
ESCAPE CRUELTY 109

DAY 17
WRITE A BIO 117

DAY 18
WIN NOBLY 125

DAY 19
EMPATHY VERSUS SPITE 135

DAY 20
THE POWER OF RESPECT 141

DAY 21
ONE THING DONE RIGHT 151

DAY 22
REJECT COMFORT MEDIA 157

DAY 23
PRACTICE SEX TRANSMUTATION 163

DAY 24
PRESENT RIGHT 171

DAY 25
LEAVE THE AIRPORT 181

DAY 26
DO YOU ENJOY SUFFERING? 185

DAY 27
YOU ARE NOT SOMEONE
ELSE'S DECISION 191

DAY 28
IS THIS NECESSARY? 195

DAY 29
CHECK YOUR VALUES 201

DAY 30
ONE MISSING THING 211

APPENDIX
*THE MIRACLE MONTH*
READING GROUP GUIDE 217

ABOUT THE AUTHOR 285

# INTRODUCTION
## "HOW SICK?"

This book is not for the meek or retiring. Or, put differently, it is for those who are tired of being so. It is for people who want to remake their lives along more powerful lines—and who are certain of that fact within their psyches.

This book is for people who would prefer nearly any alternative than to slide back into the anxiety, self-limitations, and half-in, half-out existence that they have known until now.

Does that sound extreme? It is not. It is an open door to change. Several years ago I sat in a group meeting of esoteric seekers who were rigorously dedicated to finding a new way in life. Most of the group members were well-versed in different spiritual and therapeutic traditions—but all were unsatisfied.

"I am just *so sick* of being *afraid* of everything," someone said.

"How sick?" asked a senior member of the group.

*How sick?* How sick are *you* of the same paint-by-numbers limitations, repetitive conflicts, rote thoughts, and psychological habits? Sick *enough* that you are finally, desperately ready to let them go in favor of something new? The depth of your sincerity in responding to that question determines whether you are ready for the program in this book. There is a secret to self-help: ravenous hunger for personal change. With it, everything is possible. Without it, no program will deliver you.

When I speak of letting go of the old, what do I really mean? What occurs when we discontinue or at least disrupt familiar, depleting patterns? What occurs is the only thing that can occur: wielding of power. Power, call it self-agency, is your birthright. It is bound to ethics and reciprocity, as we naturally must function as a human community, a point to which I will return.

The frustrated exercise of personal power is what sends us into endless cycles of therapy, morbid self-reflection, the same old discussions over wine with friends ("Why did he say this? What did she mean by that?"), and a spiritual search that too often counsels us to "let go" and "just be" while rarely producing results—and even eschewing the concept of results—in conduct, happiness, wellbeing, and maturity.

Ultimately, frustrated power is the only enemy you've got. Not your past or present; not your boss, unsteady mate, or depleting friends; not machinations against you; not even self-uncertainty. All of those are symptoms of frustrated power and not causes.

*The Miracle Month* is a 30-day, self-enforced academy intended to transform, disrupt, or upend the most common impediments to your power. When I use the term "miracle" I mean a fortuitous development that surpasses all reasonable circumstance and expectation. And I mean exactly that. *The Miracle Month* is not intended as a cute-sounding title but as a summons to dramatic and lasting change in your life.

This book can be read wholly on its own, but it forms a natural adjunct to my previous books *The Miracle Club* and *The Miracle Habits*. The former makes the case for how our minds change reality. The latter deals with concrete daily behaviors that foster change. Do not concern yourself if you haven't read those previous books. They are not prerequisites. But do know that we are on a 30-day journey that enlists the powers of your psyche—an amalgam of intellect and emotion—as well as your physicality. My hope is that this book proves a totalizing experience.

\*      \*      \*

Just as your thoughts, actions, and behaviors can invite catastrophes, the same factors can cultivate what I have just described as miracles. Hence, *The Miracle Month*, if followed, is intended to ignite dramatic change— and within a fixed timeframe. It is a work of urgency written at a period when psychological and material needs are acutely felt. I have dedicated myself to each of its methods both privately and in collaboration with others. Personal verification and altered conduct are the only empirical tools we possess on the path of self-development. That is why when evaluating philosophical or spiritual systems I insist on the question: "Does it work?" That is a question I will never qualify, explain away, or avoid. I believe that every practical philosophy, especially my own, must stand in service to it. Any religious or therapeutic philosophy that evades that question, either through scholasticism or deflection, has no claim on you.

This book is not specifically oriented toward money-getting, job change, finding a mate, or conventional models of success—although such things may and, in time, *should come*, if desired. Rather, *The Miracle Month* is a guide toward fully occupying yourself, toward feeling a more complete self-possession even during periods of emotional strain and failure, and those will come as certain as the cycles of day and night. But I promise that if you *authentically follow* all of the 30 daily steps in this book you will grow, expand, and experience a greatly broadened sense of personal power.

A philosopher was once asked: "Isn't everything that we need already inside of us?" He replied: "There's a lot more inside you than just that." Our task is to chip away at that problematic "more," which is to say everything superfluous and diverting, and to replace it with the crux of who we believe ourselves to be, which is probably correct. Most people feel themselves possessed of a sense of frustrated beingness. We believe that there is a truer self waiting to be born. This concept appears in many of humanity's great myths and religious parables. If that ideal is correct, as I believe it is, use this program as your guide to its near-term cultivation.

Life is generative. Barring some overwhelmingly countervailing force, such as a health crisis, you occupy a world of growth, expansion, and productivity—as well as eventual decline. Once you enter this flow, only superfluous and self-defeating actions, or a bodily automatism such as an addiction, can obstruct your role in it. Such a barrier frustrates your power-seeking impulse and results in most of what we classify as neurosis. As alluded, no amount of therapy, circuitous talking, or self-scrutiny will replace the proper exercise of your power or self-agency to foster your most valued aims in life. And such aims must be accomplished with *reciprocity*. The wholeness of life, as with the wholeness of the individual, mandates that every act gets compensated in kind. That is why bullies, cheats, and cynics are perpetually shifty, nervous, and unhappy.

The payback for your actions may not be of the *same type* but it will be exacted or rewarded on the same scale. People who are naturally empathic tend to enter life with this sensibility. I consider the cycle of reciprocity the meaning behind all ethics. I was once telling psychical researcher Dean Radin about a graphic novel that moved me in which Superman was stripped of his powers but retained his wish to carry out justice. "Does he have super emotions?" Dean asked. "He has super ethics," I replied. "Ethics," Dean said, "come from the emotions." Absolutely right. Without a fineness of sensitivity in the individual, ethics are vague, uneven, and inconsistently applied. When ethics are present—and I am not wholly sure they can be taught—the individual possesses an innate sense of reciprocity.

The exercises in this book can be started at any time. Although I speak colloquially of a month, you do not have to key this program to a calendar. I ask that you do not read ahead but allow yourself to progress through these steps on a daily basis so that they are fresh the first time you encounter them. There is a special energy in approaching a practical idea for the first time. One of the keys to succeeding in a program of self-development is the newness that you feel when discovering a method or idea, or finding a way to cultivate that sense of newness when repeating an exercise.

I also ask that you not read this book as you're settling in or drifting off at night but start early in the day, ideally first thing in the morning. These steps are action-oriented, even if sometimes in an interior way, and you'll want most of the waking day in front of you to enact them. Although each exercise or thought experiment can be commenced, and sometimes completed, in a single day, most of them require cumulative actions that extend beyond the 30-day period.

This is not a "dry" program but if you are drinking, smoking weed, or using drugs heavily enough to make you wake up later in the day than you generally want, or to cause you to routinely pop an Advil to get on with the day, then you must designate *at least* 10 days among these 30 as "clean." You can apportion those 10 days however you wish, either consecutively or nonconsecutively. That simply requires you to spend one third of this period clean. If you cannot do that, then you cannot do the program in this book.

\* \* \*

Some of what you'll find in *The Miracle Month* may seem broad and bold ("Stand for Something") and some may appear basic or domestic ("Bike Everywhere Possible"). But don't be sure in advance which is which or *what can really make a difference in your life*. We are whole beings. One change naturally ignites others. As I've explored in my previous books, there is no real boundary between "inner" and "outer"; "essence" and "personality"; "spiritual" and "material"; or "higher" and "lower." Where would one end and the other begin? Such differences are artifice. You possess a single life, which is as organically blended as the particles that compose an element. Alter one aspect and you alter all. Hence, there are no "big" or "little" steps. There is only sincerity and effort. In that vein, you will find that I am deeply self-disclosing at several points in this book; this is because we are co-seekers and I must be honest with you if I am asking you to be honest with yourself, which this program also demands.

Most of the exercises in this book do not rely on the nature of your spiritual outlook, or even having one; but in a few cases I ask you to work with what I consider extra-physical qualities of life. That is my only definition of the spiritual. In other cases, I deal directly with the overt actions and routines of daily existence, areas where we often sacrifice our true selves through rote behaviors; we rarely realize the transforming potential of a new approach to the habitual. This brings me to a final point. Nothing in this book is based in "common sense," a quality that I do not believe exists. Notice how we generally use the term to denote its absence. There is good sense, which is rare. But there is nothing common, which is to say widespread and given, about discernment and application. We possess sensory tools through which to navigate life in matters of ordinary need, but those are not inherently tools of relatability, perspicacity, and self-development. Those are things for which you must work.

I often tell people that profundity is experienced only in application. We claim to know that we shouldn't lie, trash-talk, steal, engage in blather, or misuse what belongs to another—but what does knowing matter in the absence of application? It is only when you apply a "simple" principle—and also risk failing at it—that you are placed before some of life's most vexing issues, including the rupture between intention and action. We cannot expect success at each step. Application and persistency are our guiding lights this month. It is a month worth living.

\*    \*    \*

After having received some really wonderful letters from readers of *The Miracle Month*—including pieces of graphic art inspired by the book—I am glad to be able to offer this second edition. Some readers wrote to say that they sensed they were personally on this 30-day journey with me ("this felt like a conversation between friends; encouraging and supportive yet, at times, in your face")—and that is, in fact, true. I worked through each of these steps in real time and I disclose my frank experiences with each day. In that vein, this new edition includes a reading group guide in the appendix in which I attempt to take you deeper into each day's journey. The reading group guide—which can be used by solitary readers, as well—is drawn from an online, 30-day group that I led through the book, seeker to seeker. It is my hope that reading the complementary essays keyed to each day will heighten the book's intimacy and the nature of our search together.

# DAY 1
## YOUR DAILY UNIFORM

Today, your first day, you get rid of everything—and I mean everything—superfluous in your wardrobe.

The point is to chisel down your year-round wardrobe to a simple uniform in which you feel comfortable, dynamic, functional, and relaxed. Clothing in which you feel and look your best—and which is grounded in a sense of self—affects a change throughout your being. Again, there is no such thing as "inner" and "outer" or "higher" and "lower" in our program. Those are empty designations fed to us by translations of translations of spiritual literature or hand-me-down therapeutic ideas. Life is a whole. Alter one element and you alter all of it.

In that vein, select a basic, simple wardrobe that tells your story.

I own the following items of clothing and accoutrements:

- Eighteen t-shirts (various designs, mostly black).
- Sixteen men's boxer briefs (black).
- Eight men's boot socks (mostly black).
- Three pairs of stretch denim jeans (black).
- Three leather jackets for different weather (black).
- Two different weights of leather winter gloves (one black, one camo).
- A camo winter coat.
- A zip-up bomber jacket for winter biking.
- A replica of the tuxedo/shirt/shoes in which Elvis Presley got married. (You need a tux from time to time.)
- One pair of Doc Marten boots. (Sex Pistols collaboration limited edition.)
- One pair of Reyes boxing boots (black).
- One pair of Palladium boots (black).
- One pair of Chuck Taylor-style water shoes (black).
- One leather belt (guess which color?).
- One winter hat with ear flaps (the Japanese cartoon dinosaur Domo appears on it).
- One pair of prescription sunglasses (replica of those worn by Kurt Russell in John Carpenter's biopic *Elvis*).

- One pair of prescription eyeglasses (matte black frames).
- Three pairs of yoga pants (black).
- One pair of camo sweats.
- One all-season scarf from Italy.
- A red tartan wallet and chain.
- A bathing suit (black) and camo bathing trunks.
- Two silver bracelets. (I own no wristwatch.)
- A black Nehru suit and shirt. (I never wear it. It's my guilt item, of which you're permitted one.)
- A leather shirt (black).
- A quilted, winter-weight shirt for layering (navy—my break with habit).
- An Army surplus backpack used for work and travel (black).

That's it. And it's more than I need 90 percent of the time.

Now, my clothing choices are specific to my gender, taste, activities, and work. You may face different circumstances based on climate, comfort, employment, artistic needs, and so on. You may live within a different stylistic sphere. That is natural. More important than my choices are your own—assert your self-expressiveness with simplicity and decision.

In 2019, I told the following to the fashion website *Orttu*:

I would say that no single, unilateral step has made me personally happier in life than dressing and adorning myself exactly as I want. Anton LaVey (a very under-appreciated magical intellect), called it part of creating one's "total environment." I think spiritual leaders and therapists inadvertently mislead people, and themselves, by undervaluing aesthetics and personal agency. By modeling how you want to be seen in the world you also heighten your sense of self in myriad ways, including the creative, relational, and sexual.

I have come to understand fashion more fully as a spiritual field—by spiritual I mean extra-physical. We're taught to think of beauty as something ephemeral. But I believe it's much more than that. Beauty, design, and curation alter people's lives—they feed every aspect of the human experience. Without such things, life is nothing but labor and survival. I think this is why most people in the fashion world are quite spiritual if not religious. It's why much of our fashion echoes archetypal images, devotional art, and occult symbolism. Fashion is, in its way, a window to the beyond.

There is a further dimension to paying attention to matters of dress, uniform, and adornment. This was brought home to me by legendary basketball coach John Wooden, who I had the opportunity to interview six years before he died at age 99 in 2010. Wooden had led UCLA to an unprecedented ten NCAA championships, including seven in a row. Each season on the first day of practice he told his hotshot recruits: "Gentleman, today we're going to figure out how to put our shoes and socks on." Some players blanched. Wooden calmly explained that most players are benched for blisters, and that the easiest way to avoid them is to pay attention to the basics.

He then meticulously showed them how to roll up their socks and tighten their laces. "I wanted it done consciously, not quickly or casually," he told me. "Otherwise we would not be doing everything possible to prepare in the best way."

Now, my motives differ from Wooden's. But only in part. By maximizing performance, confidence, and, in this case, self-image, you place yourself in greater control of all factors that *can be controlled*.

How you feel on the outside—which is easier to manage when you keep choices minimal, simple, and integral—impacts and mirrors how you feel within. All of life converges. Hence the value I place on so-called small things—in this case how you comport yourself without. This step begins the person you are becoming in these 30 days.

# DAY 2
## GIVE IN

There are times to fight. But on this day we are going to discover the power of backing down from a fight.

I do not mean that in some ironic way, although I realize that it may sound surprising given the damn-the-torpedoes tone that I take at some points in this book. The fact is: conflicts are extremely draining. The ancient martial text *The Art of War* cautions against leaving a "standing army in the field"—it is exhausting, vulnerable, and dangerous.

I ask you this day to select *one conflict in your life*, whether current or persistent, of-the-moment or years-old, and just check out of it. Unilaterally surrender. Back down. Walk away.

In every conflict someone must finally give in. Why not you? Often the person who prevails in life is the one who is wise enough and strong enough to backdown and step away from time to time. *The Art of War* counsels that you should never fight unless victory is assured.

Try as we might to control things, and self-possessed as we usually are of the rightness of our position (although this sensibility is often based on past emotions and events and not necessarily on present circumstances), we cannot always foresee what is winnable or worth it. Sometimes we lose or we experience what is perceived as a loss until later reassessment. In any case, costs are deepened and worsened if we persist after an obvious benefit is lost or is minor. Do not fight simply out of visceral desire for dominance.

Some losses are better than victory. Consider what is at stake. By backing down you may preserve the comity of a key relationship. That's more significant than prevailing in a narrow material matter. In a more general sense, let's say that you are wrongly charged or overcharged for some item or service. Sometimes taking the hit is preferable to investing hours to make it right, even if the charge is unfair. What value do you place on your time, energy, quality of life, and health? What other kinds of things can you be doing than fighting? Sometimes stepping away is the better of the two options.

One time my health-insurance carrier ripped me off for $900. They refused to reimburse me for some prescriptions that were clearly covered during a time gap in which I was switching plans. I made multiple calls, sat on the phone, and filed and then refiled claims. Three separate times the insurer used coding schemes—basically a bureaucratized and obfuscating system of fraud—to deny my coverage. Coverage for which I had paid. Nonetheless, I could see where this was headed. Insurance companies routinely use coding to delay or deny policyholders coverage to which they are entitled. This is among the reasons why I call private health insurers organized crime with a refrigerator magnet. It is no joke and, unfortunately, little exaggeration.

For all that, I dropped it. I made the judgment to save myself potentially hours sitting on hold with a customer service rep who is as helpless to affect policy as a buck private during trench warfare. I elected not to invest further time and stress in refiling the same claims, all of which would probably get returned with some new denial. The fact is, once you are denied coverage, unless you get very lucky or have a corporate HR officer, a contracted advocate, or someone who can personally intervene (I was self-insured at the time) the health insurer will use its bureaucratic machinery to grind you down. So, I decided to take the hit. I was able to at the time and I felt I had to dedicate my energies to deadlines, my kids, and other matters.

I was later glad I did so because, at least as of this writing, some of the money came back to me in an unexpected way. Sometimes life evens out through byways that cannot be foreseen. I also averted a lot of stress. Ethically, the insurer was wrong. But correcting that wrong required activity on a larger scale than I was willing to engage.

I have faced struggles over greater sums of money. In 2020, an educational institution owed me a much-needed refund for a canceled program for one of my children during the Covid crisis. I felt that they made the refund process overly complex and slow, dividing the refund into sums payable over several months. I could no longer contest the charge with my credit card company because too much time had passed. After some friction, I decided to drop the issue. For one thing, I didn't want a protracted dispute to cloud my kids' experience if they returned to the program. To my pleasant surprise, however, some weeks after backing down the full sum did arrive. Maybe I was first in line because of the alarms I sounded earlier or maybe something just worked out.

This raises another dimension to what I've been describing. Lost battles are sometimes quietly won battles. I believe that life is compensatory. As occurred with my insurance carrier, compensation can arrive quickly and clearly, or other times it may arrive indirectly and inscrutably. In any case, experience and observation have taught me to believe in the Hermetic principle that every event is mirrored by an equal and opposite one. Everything occurs in rhythmic motion along a sliding scale. One action naturally evokes its opposite, even if we do not always have perspective to see it. This is among the meanings of the Hermetic maxim, "As above, so below." Ralph Waldo Emerson wrote a wonderful essay on the topic, "Compensation"—I think it is the closest thing we possess to a fully encompassing philosophy of life. I reread it at least once a year. I ask you to read it or begin reading it today.

What I am describing occurs in concentrically expansive ways. The cycle of compensation is why some events that you look back on as defeats or humiliations have produced in you traits of maturity and resiliency. The traits of which you are most proud probably arose from periods of pain or adversity. Scan your life for this. It is why Nietzsche wrote in 1888 in *Twilight of the Idols*: "*Out of life's school of war*: What does not destroy me, makes me stronger." That aphorism, perhaps overused or seemingly overstated, is no false truism—if you understand the mechanics at the back of it. Adversity harbors a kind of deliverance and protection. Recognize this and you set in motion the natural processes of compensation. You also save yourself from a good deal of inner turmoil.

I would be remiss if I did not add that some fights cannot be backed off from. These are fights that are sprung upon you with repetition and must be settled. When someone in your life repeatedly draws you into conflict—we will examine escaping such people in mid-month—you may find yourself compelled to mount resistance or be consumed. As will be explored, the one true victory in such cases is eliminating the relationship altogether. We will get there. For today, however, I ask that you select one conflict in your life in which the payoff or spoils are questionable and: drop it. The experience will prove repeatable.

# DAY 3
## APOLOGIZE AND MEAN IT

Whether it is today or sometime before this 30-day period ends, you must apologize to someone who is owed it—and do so sincerely.

An apology, either spoken or written, must be *without qualification*. Few things in human relations are worse than saying, "I'm sorry if you felt . . ." or "I'm sorry if you were offended . . ." That is an additional injury because *it simply blames the other person for oversensitivity*. Plausible denial is the most common tool used by psychological bullies and aggressors. A nearly equal runner up is, "I'm sorry, but you also . . ." A real apology seeks no concessions, even if they are justified. Sometimes you may have injured a person who is not blameless him or herself. For example, you may have overreacted to someone who hurt you. An apology doesn't necessarily mean that you've absolved the other party of all obligation. It means that *you accept the full burden and reckoning of your own performance in the matter.* This is why apologies must be unilateral.

Real apologies are rare. Has anyone ever apologized to you *without qualification*? Have you done so for another?

The fact is, all of us hurt one another all the time. This often occurs in subtle ways but sometimes through overt aggression. Again, the harm may be an act of over-compensation for a preceding or adjunct wrong. But if you can bring yourself to apologize *without* asking for something in exchange you break the pattern of repetitive emotional violence. Anger only begets further anger, offense further offense. Whether the other person ought to reflect on his or her own instigating actions is beside the point; and you have provided the best possible chance for that to occur.

When you sincerely apologize you also announce a set of standards for yourself. You declare yourself someone who is capable of accountability. People note that.

Personally, I have sometimes used an angry or confrontative tone with people who I thought were playing loose with money, facts, or sincerity. When I reflect back on such matters, I usually apologize. Because my apology signals what I regard as the proper baseline for *my own* behavior. As alluded, apologies cannot enforce ethics and do not compel others to self-correct. An apology is not the enforcement of standards on anyone but myself.

Bear in mind, too, that people always remember when they've been insulted or humiliated without recourse. *The wounded party remembers such an incident a lot longer than the offender does.* The injured person will likely hold a grudge, which may get settled at a surprising moment. The escape hatch from that dynamic of retribution is a sincere apology.

Above all, an apology is an ethical imperative. Even if the harm is hidden or unlikely to extract a cost, you apologize because, as noted in the introduction, life is reciprocal. Pay your debts. That is the heart of all ethics.

So long as you apologize in a meaningful way, it doesn't matter whether you say it face to face, on the phone, or by text or messaging. What matters only is that you go all the way.

I am not asking you to review the pages of your life and make a broad confessional or seek serial absolution. You probably cannot recall the various people you've hurt, anyway. Rather, I am asking you to do this *once* during this 30-day period—if not today then certainly before you are done. Get the feeling of apologizing and know how to repeat it.

It is entirely up to the other person whether to accept your apology. Which brings up a related point: *you are not asking forgiveness*. Forgiveness should never be asked for since, like offering a qualified apology, doing so displaces responsibility onto the other person. Asking forgiveness places the other party into a subtle trap since your request puts him or her to the test rather than you. (On Day 15 we are going to take a hard and fresh look at forgiveness.) All you can do is acknowledge your part in another's wound.

Your apology probably will—and almost certainly should be—made privately in order to avoid embarrassing the other party. But you may find a situation where you cannot reach out to someone. Perhaps the person is deceased, has blocked you, or has asked not to be contacted (which should always be respected). I often discover that when I am writing a section of a book I receive propitiously timed messages or emails from readers which seem to address exactly what I am working on. I want to offer one such letter and my reply, which spoke to the very situation I just described. Although the letter is used with permission, I have cut the name and locale to respect the privacy of all concerned. Otherwise this is a complete and candid exchange.

Hello Mitch,

I recently discovered you through Duncan Trussell's podcast and have begun reading your book, which I'm enjoying a whole lot. I feel like the many ways you have of addressing what I've usually found to be really esoteric and detached ideas feels very real to me. It's because of this that I wanted to write and ask you a question.

This question is very hard for me to talk about. It's not that I don't want to talk about it, in fact it's always on my mind, but I feel like whenever I see people speak on similar subjects what they say isn't enough or it hasn't felt like the right place or person for me to ask. So please forgive me if I don't say things as nicely as I should, I'm just out of practice on the subject.

About two years ago I hurt someone very badly. What I did was entirely my fault. At the time though I was acting from a fear place and did what I think many people do, and that is, they try and rationalize it and explain all the reasons why it wasn't their fault. And it was easy for me to do this because the person I hurt just wasn't a very nice person. They themselves were abusive and self-centered, and I used this as an excuse to justify my actions.

In the time since I did this a lot has happened. Many people learned about what I did, and rightly, they spoke out against me. It was humiliating and awful to be outed publicly. And for a long time it only made me kick my heels in further, because I wanted to spend all this time going, well yeah I did that BUT LOOK HOW BAD THEY ARE. It took me a long time to accept my responsibility. And now, due to life circumstances, there is no way that I can apologize to this person.

I feel like I see a lot of teachers talking about how to forgive others, and how to keep yourself from giving any more energy from those that hurt you. But what do you do when you yourself have done the hurting? What do you do when you are the villain? So far the only thing that's kind of worked is meditating on my past actions. I feel like when I view them and ask for forgiveness and love, I feel great in the moment and at peace with myself, but when I go back out in the world and am confronted by people who know me by my reputation I feel crumpled and filled with grief and sorrow and self-hatred all over again. I want to change as a person. I don't want to erase my past, but how do I build a stronger me that can function at a higher level while still carrying this burden?

Anyway, I hope this all made sense and it's not too much of a bother for me to ask you.

Yours, _____

Hi _____,

I think you've come to a good place if you can acknowledge—as you do here—that you need to apologize even if the other person has serious flaws and faults. An apology must be absolutely unqualified. It doesn't mean that the other party is "off the hook" for his or her own behavior. You write here that you cannot apologize due to life circumstances. I understand that and I've been there. I suggest that you handwrite a letter of sincere apology to that person and keep it tucked away somewhere. The very act of writing that letter, and making it a tactile, by-hand letter, may have greater effects than at first appear. Your own letter to me is very well timed. I am writing a new book called *The Miracle Month* in which Day 3—in a passage that I just drafted earlier today—is about making an unqualified apology. I wonder if I could have permission to reproduce your letter in the book without any identifying characteristics, if you so wish? I respect your privacy and choice either way; but somehow this might be a fitting capstone to your situation insofar as what you've learned will shine a light for others. Every stick has two ends, as a great man once said. This may be the other end.

Very best, -Mitch-

\*      \*      \*

To recap, an apology must be unilateral. You are not asking for anything—even forgiveness. You are offering something. If you cannot contact someone, for whatever reason, handwrite a short, sincere letter of apology and tuck it away someplace private. I believe in writing down intimate statements, aims, and commitments in a tactile manner and not on a computer or device. The writing out of a statement affects a change, however small, in your world. It alters your surroundings. Although the estranged party may never see the letter, I believe that we are all bound by ties that exceed obvious sensory experience. What is spirituality but extra-physicality? I cannot codify this for you in exact terms, at least not in this book, but I do believe that the writing of such a statement makes a real difference.

I purposely placed this step early in the program so that you have no immediate time pressure in which to accomplish it—but you must accomplish it within these 30 days. And when you do you will understand the leavening and power that it brings.

# DAY 4

## BIKE EVERYWHERE POSSIBLE

n the introduction I wrote that this book deals with both psyche and physicality. The two are not really different. Today we explore that. As soon as practicable, I want you to get a bike—nothing fancy, it can be any old clunker (and is probably better that way)— and bike *everywhere possible*: to work, home, shopping (you've heard of a backpack right?). And do so wherever you live and in every kind of season and weather.*

Wear a helmet. Use lights (a must at night). And look sharp.

---

* If you have a physical challenge that makes biking untenable or impossible I ask that you substitute, to the greatest degree possible, other forms of self-propelled transportation, including a hand-cranked bike or wheelchair. In such cases, adjust the physical requirements in this chapter to fit your needs.

It will change your life.

Part of what makes us weak, conventional, slovenly, boring, and typical is that we persuade ourselves that we must use certain mechanisms to get through life, generally those that everybody else uses and that we are conditioned to use by convention. In matters of transit that often means a car. Hence, we grow accustomed to ready warmth, dryness, door-to-door convenience, and digital music or radio noise. (Have you noticed how many people leave on their radio permanently, even making guest passengers speak over it?)

In winters, many people warm their cars before entering them as though even a few minutes of less-than-optimal comfort is intolerable. We grow stiff and inflexible behind the wheel. We gain weight, get easily winded, and lose muscle. We also force ourselves into company that we may not want, such as on commutes or in carpools. None of it is strictly necessary (at least most of the time, depending on your commute and living situation), and little of it is healthy.

If you bike everywhere—and in nearly every kind of weather—you will not only become more physically resilient but, I believe, also more compelling as a person. Watch and see. You will stand out because you carry your own weight, literally and figuratively. You eschew convenience in favor of health, experience (you see and learn more about your surroundings by cycling), and greater personal freedom, coming and going at will. You will be physically tougher. You will sometimes get caught in rain and snow. Well, wet clothes and shoes dry. Cold limbs and extremities warm. Aches and pains are signs of burgeoning strength. This is not some bubblegum, uber-menschen ideal. It is the truth.

As I am writing these words I am drying out after biking in a thunderous and massive downpour over the Williamsburg Bridge, which connects Brooklyn to the Lower East Side of Manhattan. I walked into my destination soaked through as though I had jumped in a lake fully clothed. Literally. I thought: *good*. I did the very thing that I am asking you to do. If I didn't, what would that make me? I felt alive, fully enjoying the warmth of recovering, and feeling like I earned my glass of whiskey. I also earned the writing of this counsel.

If you haven't biked in a while, begin incrementally and easily. The point is not to blow your joints or take a spill but to gradually accustom yourself to a new way of life.

I recommend using a fixed or single-gear bike. Unless you are cycling in mountainous areas you can do nearly everything on a single-gear bike that you can on a multiple-gear bike. It will be more difficult at first, but you will get used to it—and you will also get stronger faster. A fixed-gear bike is generally cheaper and easier to maintain and repair than a multiple-gear bike. Also unless you opt for an expensive bike, gears can be wonky.

I bought the fixed-gear bike I currently use in 2016 for $256.16. Not a bad price. Since then I've probably spent at least the same amount on repairs and the replacement of a stolen front wheel (also get a good lock, which can run $50). I spent $42.99 on a helmet (there are cheaper models), which is absolutely vital. I recently sunk $119 into an additional lightweight, foldable helmet because it's an excellent model that I want available to my kids and that I can carry with me when traveling. I have flipped backwards on my bike and felt the rear of my head go *clunk* on the pavement. I walked away shaken but completely unharmed. Without a helmet I would have suffered a concussion, fracture, or worse. I never ride, even for a block, without a helmet. I will not permit anyone I love to do so.

This brings me to another point: motorized bikes. I oppose them. Not only do they abrogate the healthfully and environmentally sound purpose of biking but they are dangerous to pedestrians, cyclists, and their own riders, especially in urban environments. In the story I just told, I flipped over because I swerved to avoid a motorized bike. I was nearing a large puddle on a New York City bike path while a motorized bike was coming straight toward me at a faster speed than is allowable on city bike paths; I misjudged how quickly the driver would be upon me, crunched my brakes, and flipped over in an effort to avoid impact. As I write these words in July 2020, two New Yorkers just died following accidents on mopeds that belong to a rideshare service. Biking means biking. It doesn't require "improving." However careful you are, of course, biking carries risks, as do most means of transportation. Be mindful, be careful, use aggressive good sense.

I want to close this short section on a more personal note. I realize how arbitrary it can seem to tell someone to go ride a bike. But I want to share one further observation. When I bought my bike, as mentioned, it was in September of 2016. I was facing a difficult stage in life. I was transitioning out of a longtime publishing job and, not long after, out of my former marriage.

It was a harrowing but also meaningful time. I felt nervousness but also a sense of portent and possibility. Some of the blossoming I experienced coincided with—and in certain ways was abetted by—my decision to ride. Riding gave me a feeling of liberation and selfhood; it reconnected me with street culture in New York City, where biking forms a kind of anyone-can-join fraternity. (This is true in many towns and cities.) It may sound like a stretch, but I felt a return to my punk roots. It was like I was fully breathing again. The feeling proved enduring.

I am not saying that the psychological dimensions of what I described are universal—but nor do I consider my life exceptional. We are all connected in experience, as are the constituent parts of our lives. At the start of this section I wrote that biking would "change your life." I would never make such a statement in a trifling way. You will find something more than you expect.

# DAY 5
## FACE YOUR ANGER

P robably nothing costs us more in life than displays of anger, whether outbursts, rhetorical questions, biting sarcasm, or glares. People will never say it, they may not even acknowledge it to themselves, but when you direct anger towards them they are made to feel afraid and resentful and they lose trust and faith in you as a person. They will part with you at the first possible opportunity. What's more, they will imitate your behavior and direct it back at you or toward another.

I write this because I have been that angry person. I have evaluated the consequences and, as alluded, I cannot imagine that my life is radically different from anyone else's. Hence, your task today—which I am performing with you as I write these words—is to *face and acknowledge your own anger*, in whatever expression it takes, and understand its consequences.

I offer no fantasies about controlling your emotions. The mind and the emotions run on separate tracks and no amount of mental resolve will wholly bring the emotions to heel. For one thing, the emotions run faster than the intellect. You experience a pang of fear, rush of anger, or sting of resentment before you can properly evaluate it. Fear is probably the trigger for most angry or destructive emotions. And the fear response gets "wired" into us, both conditionally and physiologically, almost as fully as a bodily organ. Hence, I place relatively little faith in regulation of emotions, though I certainly recognize the efficacy of certain cognitive tools.

Rather, I suggest pitting one emotion (or maybe even the same emotion) against another. Doing so requires coming to terms with the consequences of anger. If you can clearly see the consequences that in itself may be the emotional pivot that allows you to come to terms with and curb outer displays of anger. Understanding the cost of anger may in itself rightly cause you to experience fear, sorrow, empathy, and remorse. Good. One emotion can counter another, including the display of anger. You'll notice I am saying "display." This is an outside-inside exercise. We are often taught that intention precedes act. I am not sure that is so. It is not always easy to trace the ignition point of anger or fear; we sometimes feel such emotions first physiologically, either based on memories or our mind-body makeup, and we then select a target after the fact. Hence, the "cause" is not always as important as it seems. Our object here is to interrupt the display.

In order to help you explore, acknowledge, and alter your expressions of anger I am going to share with you a very personal note that I produced recent to this writing. This is a letter I sent to one of my children while he was away at a wilderness camp. I wrote this letter at the urging of a therapist, to whom I am grateful. (I don't want anyone to feel that I do not honor modern therapeutic and spiritual counseling.) I believe that by sharing this note, personal as it is—*and I must emphasize that I disclose details only about myself and not another*—you may recognize within it the common crisis of anger.

Dear _____,

I hope you are doing well. I wanted to write you about something very personal today which I haven't fully expressed before. One of the greatest regrets of my life—and something that I personally want to apologize to you for—is that I displayed a lot of anger at home when you were young.

To be honest, I have struggled with anger issues all of my life. I felt a great deal of pressure from parenting, and at the same time starting my writing career, and I allowed that to erupt into angry displays. I think my anger was unintentionally passed on to you and your brother as an acceptable form of behavior. But I have finally learned over the past few years—belatedly—the terrible impact that anger has on other people. When I behave with anger, it may, for the moment, appear to get me what I want; but in a fuller and more long-term way it causes other people to lose faith in me. When I act out in anger it makes other people afraid—maybe it made you afraid—and they feel resentful and want to get away from me at the first possible opportunity.

I think when I was young I felt that anger won me some short-term "victories," and I made the really huge mistake, as many people do, of believing that anger is some kind of a strength. It is not. It breeds mistrust, resentment, and a lack of faith in the angry person. That is the legacy I must deal with.

I am so, so sorry for the times I erupted in and displayed anger. I cannot promise that I will never again slip, which would be unrealistic, but I do promise that I will always try not to slide in that direction. And if I do, I want you to call me out on it. You are entitled never to experience anger from me.

You never fully know what a situation will be like until you are in it. I thought parenting would be easier for me than it turned out to be. I thought that I would take more naturally to it. But after you and your brother were born, as much as I loved you then and today, I found it very difficult to parent, hold down my job, and embark on my writing career. The demands sometimes felt overwhelming. Also, I felt unhappy with certain lifestyle choices that just seemed to creep up. That, too, resulted in my behaving angrily probably as a way of dealing with anxiety, stress, and unhappiness. Again, it was entirely wrong on my part. But I fear that I communicated to you and to your brother that anger is appropriate or "grownup." I certainly came to believe that when I was young based upon my own father's behavior.

Today I am dedicated never to displaying that to you again.

Much love and speak soon,

Dad

I ask you today to write your own letter of this nature. Make it starkly honest. I provided my disclosure to abet that. Your letter need look nothing like mine. But, above all: take responsibility. (If you need guidance refer back to Day 3: *Apologize and Mean It*.) I encourage you to send this letter to whomever you choose to address. *But that last step is not strictly necessary*; you may choose to write it to someone who would rather not be contacted or who may be deceased, such as a parent. The important thing is simply to write it and mean it.

We cannot necessarily redress the past but a change in perspective resonates with greater breadth and impact than may initially appear. A great teacher once observed: The past controls the future, but the present controls the past.

When you acknowledge your anger and understand what it has meant you set to flight a possibility that is unseen. That is today's mission.

# DAY 6
## STAND FOR SOMETHING

Your social, cultural, and political opinions do not matter. Everyone has them, informed or not. Your principles, however, *do* matter.

Today I want you to identify what you are willing to make a sacrifice for. What you *really* believe in. Not what you tweet about. Political tweets are generally consequence-free and results-free forms of self-aggrandizement. They say nothing about what, if anything, you would sacrifice in income, friends, or even personal safety if put to the test.

In early 2020, I resolved to stop tweeting about politics because it only results in contest and anger. But that doesn't meant that I will not publicly stand for my beliefs. My core belief is in the sanctity of the individual search. I will not compromise the boundaryless nature of my search, which also forms the basis for what I write and speak about. I am not a teacher, life coach, self-help maven, or guru. I am a seeker. Hence, if I do not share my search I abrogate the basis of my work.

Regarding the search, I do not take an "anything goes" approach absent discernment. For example, I reject the perpetual hunt for an enemy—humanity's oldest motive following procreation and subsistence—which is at the heart of most of what is called conspiracy theorizing. Conspiracism is not a real search but the playing out of an ancient spasm in which an imagined adversary—whether witches of the Middle Ages or fictitious "Satanists" in the minds of QAnon followers—is generally located among the innocent and easily isolated.

Nor do I believe in subjecting others to the consequences of my search. I claim an absolute right only to inner experiment whose results I personally shoulder. I reject non-provoked violence and honor reciprocal ethics. "Thou shalt leave another alone," is a guiding principle.

For that approach to the search I claim near-total freedom—both for myself and you.

Reciprocity sometimes requires speaking out against injustice as I perceive it. In October of 2020 I published a dissenting article about the life of professional skeptic James Randi who died that month. Amid a near-total uniformity of media tributes, I felt it necessary to document an unpopular but compelling truth: that the famous debunker of psychical claims had himself degraded authentic skepticism and open inquiry by routinely misrepresenting and smearing key figures and their research within the academic study of ESP.

The piece met with a good deal of support—as well as a chorus of vituperative and, in some cases, coordinated attacks, a Randian tactic that I expected. In "The Man Who Destroyed Skepticism," which appeared at *Boing Boing* on October 26, 2020, I wrote the following with examples, sources, and citations in the full piece:

> Last week marked the death at age 92 of James "The Amazing" Randi, a stage magician who became internationally famous as a skeptic—indeed Randi rebooted the term "skepticism" as a response to the boom in psychical claims and research in the post-Woodstock era. Today, thousands of journalists, bloggers, and the occasional scientist call themselves skeptics in the mold set by Randi. Over the past decade, the investigator himself was heroized in documentaries, profiles, and, now, obituaries. A *Guardian* columnist eulogized him as the "prince of reason."

I mourn Randi's passing for those who loved him, and there were many. But his elevation to the Mount Rushmore of skepticism obfuscates a basic truth. In the end, the feted researcher was no skeptic. He was to skepticism what Senator Joseph McCarthy was to anticommunism—a showman, a bully, and, ultimately, the very thing he claimed to fight against: a fraud. This has corroded our intellectual culture—in a Trumpian age when true skepticism is desperately needed . . .

As a historian and writer on metaphysical topics, I have spent time among fraudulent mediums, and I share Randi's outrage at their manipulations. I have no issue with his or others' targeting of stage psychics and woo-woo con artists—I join in it. But Randi made his name, and influenced today's professional skeptics, by smearing the work of serious researchers, such as [J.B.] Rhine, who, in founding the original parapsychological lab at Duke with his wife and co-researcher Louisa, labored intensively— and in a scientifically conservative manner that reverse-mirrored Randi's work—to devise research protocols for testing psychical phenomena . . .

Randi proved hugely adept at sound bites. Most researchers and scientists do poorly with sound bites. Such devices contributed to his being lionized in news coverage by observers who seemed genuinely unaware of his unwillingness to distinguish between parapsychologists who perform juried and meticulous work . . . versus the average storefront psychic. The "broad smear" and polarized thinking typify most professional skepticism today.

Indeed, when encountering the efforts of clinicians . . . Randi often played "move the goalpost." Physicists Bruce Rosenblum and Fred Kuttner made this pertinent historical observation in their book *Quantum Enigma: Physics Encounters Consciousness*: "Greek science had a fatal flaw. *It had no mechanism to compel consensus*. The Greeks saw experimental tests of scientific conclusions as no more relevant than were experimental tests of political or aesthetic positions. Conflicting views could be argued indefinitely." Randi and his admirers embraced this flaw as a polemical device, often wearing down scientists and winning over journalists with perpetual, repeat-loop disparagement of ESP research and other science they disfavored, no matter how valid the methods . . .

I sympathize with those who want to challenge credulity and generalized references to psychical phenomena—and all the more with researchers and investigators who expose frauds. I sympathize, too, with those who have lost a man, a friend, and a spouse. But to the intellectual community, and anyone concerned with critical inquiry in general, Randi's legacy should serve as a cautionary tale and a call to restore sound practices when discussing or writing about contentious topics in science or any field. These are things that a showman can deter but never erase.

Now, I am not asking you to agree with my perspective, which you can evaluate in the larger piece and the nature of the rejoinders to it. I am asking you to have your own perspective on *what matters to you*. And by having a point of view, I mean *identifying what matters enough* that to defend or pursue it you are willing to shed some of the familiar comforts of career, money, or social approbation.

Depending on your outlook, this is not necessarily a big ask, since here in the U.S. we still dwell in a society where controversial speech—as compared to some other nations—does not routinely result in loss of livelihood or freedoms, although I encourage no one to take such liberties lightly or for granted, especially with the rise of ultra-irrationalism in the form of the aforementioned QAnon and related movements. Indeed, we've witnessed far too many exceptions and downward slopes to assume that the normative protections of expression are unshakable. They are not. You help to protect such things by *using them*. Writing about principles of free expression in a general way, or tweeting out your point of view from an air-conditioned home or from behind the anonymity of an account name, does little to forward the cause of expressiveness. Expression is in use—or it is a facade.

To express something that really matters, ask yourself today: *What do I stand for?* Write down the answer. And make sure you mean it. One act of dishonesty will abrogate this entire program. Once you know what you stand for, *constructively act on it,* if not today then within the timeframe of this program. Your act will both add to your sense of self-establishment and shine a light for others.

Soon after writing this segment, I encountered this piece of decal art on a mailbox at the corner of Ridge and Stanton Streets around the block from where I lived while writing this book on New York's Lower East Side. What does it mean to you?

# DAY 7
## KEEP YOUR WORD

W e live in a world where people break their word—to keep an engagement, to finish a chore, to meet a deadline, to pay a bill on time—for nearly any reason or mild inconvenience. Such acts erode basic bonds of trust.

I once had to move apartments quickly and a friend who committed to helping me pulled out at the last moment because his knees were acting up. Well, okay . . . but in such a case the person could still come and help pack boxes, roll up wires, take down the shower curtain, order pizza. A philosopher I know once said: "The only real emergency is a medical emergency." If you agree to be somewhere, do something, or meet a deadline, you must do it, barring a health emergency. If you cannot stand by your word you cannot do anything of value in life.

New Age culture is full of people who announce themselves the reincarnate of the Delphic oracle or as channels for an immortal intelligence yet who fail the most basic tests of life: showing up on time, being accountable, and keeping commitments. *You cannot be powerful unless you keep your word.*

In his haunting 1964 memoir *Boyhood with Gurdjieff*, novelist Fritz Peters (1913–1979) recounted the commitment exacted from him by the Greek-Armenian spiritual teacher G.I. Gurdjieff (1866–1949) when Fritz was 11-years-old. The adolescent met Gurdjieff in June 1924 when he was sent to spend the summer at the teacher's school, the Prieuré, a communal estate in Fontainebleau-Avon outside of Paris. Speaking to Fritz on a stone patio one day, Gurdjieff banged the table with his fist and asked, "Can you promise to do something for me?"

The boy gave a firm, "Yes."

The teacher gestured to the estate's vast expanse of lawns. "You see this grass?" he asked.

"Yes," Fritz said again.

"I give you work. You must cut this grass, with machine, every week."

Fritz agreed—but that wasn't enough. Gurdjieff "struck the table with his fist for the second time. 'You must promise on your God.' His voice was deadly serious. 'You must promise that you will do this thing no matter what happens.'"

Fritz replied, "I promise."

Again, not enough. "Not just promise," Gurdjieff said. "Must promise you will do no matter what happens, no matter who try stop you. Many things can happen in life."

Fritz vowed again.

*Many things can happen in life.* Very soon, in the lives of Fritz and his teacher, something seismic and upending did occur. Gurdjieff suffered a severe car accident and for several weeks laid in a near-coma recovering at the Prieuré. Fritz, feeling that the whole thing seemed almost foreordained, honored his commitment to keep mowing the lawns. But he met with stern resistance. Several adults at the school insisted to him that the noise would disturb Gurdjieff's convalescence and could even result in the master's death. Fritz recalled how unsparingly the promise had been exacted and how fully it had been given. He refused to relent. He kept mowing—and no one physically stopped him. One day while Fritz was cutting the lawns he spied the recovering master smile at him from his bedroom window.

\*　　\*　　\*

Obviously most commitments do not involve life or death situations. But how can we possibly expect to rise to situations that really do matter—and how can we always know which really matter—when we cannot honor our commitments on a smaller scale?

We fool ourselves about our abilities and solidity. We typically think, "Well when it *really counts,* I will step up." That kind of belief is untested. Who we are in small matters is who we are entirely, a point to which we return on Day 21. Most of the time small matters are our *only* proving ground. For example, someone who lies in seemingly small things will lie in large things. A person who proves reliable or unreliable in small matters will follow through on up the scale.

Your task on Day 7 is simple: *Keep your word in every matter, large or small.*

If you are meeting someone at 1 p.m. today show up on time. If you have a phone call or Zoom session be there on the hour, not two minutes after the hour while everyone waits for you. If you owe a sum of money, pay it, to the greatest extent possible, right now. If you are lending someone your car, do so in earnest—not with the fuel gauge on reserve.

Most of us lack the ability to keep our word. *But we do not know that because we do not test ourselves.* It is easier to minimize a circumstance or rationalize an excuse than to face the truth, which is that we are thrown off course by the mildest turn in the road. But that's what life consists of: turns in the road. Something unexpected almost always occurs. Are you a real person if something small abrogates your ability to follow through?

Few things will bring you greater trust from another and *from yourself* than keeping your word and following through.

The education that Fritz Peters received as an adolescent can rarely, if ever, be replicated in our world today. But we can at least honor the principle involved. If I find myself unable to fulfill the principle, and if I am self-honest about it, that too is valuable. I would rather fail a hundred times over than hide from failure. The impression of one's inability holds an immensely valuable lesson in itself.

# DAY 8
## WHAT DO YOU WANT?

N ow that we've explored some key emotional, ethical, and lifestyle issues, I am going to ask perhaps the most important question facing you: *What do you want in life?*

Many of us in the West occupy such a gratification-oriented society, or at least we did pre-Covid, that that question can seem almost banal. It is not. The truth is, that question gets stolen from you all the time.

It gets stolen in this way. I once described to a trusted and capable therapist what I wanted in life. "But that's superficial," he replied. I wasn't shaken or angered by his answer. Because I believed in my own. I replied, "Listen, you've known me for a long time. Do you *really* think that's superficial? Or do you think

perhaps that I have wrestled with that question, ethically and practically, and emerged with the intimate
acknowledgment that this is, in fact, what I really want?
And if what I've just described is true, how can it be
defined as superficial?"

I want you to be free to make this inquiry for yourself: *What do you want*? That is your project on Day 8.
This question and its response belong to you alone.

Now, you may not always be able to *get* what you
want, at least not in the form you expect. Indeed, I've
often received what I wanted through channels that
I never expected or could have foreseen. But never
allow yourself not to *know what that something is* and to
acknowledge it. I believe that mature men and women
are capable of knowing what they want without inter-
mediaries or someone else reconditioning or reframing
their wish, a point to which I'll return. I think that
too many ministers or teachers assume that unless an
answer falls within certain hallowed (I would say habitual) boundaries it must somehow be illusory, socially
proscribed, narrow, or the result of misunderstanding.
But what if none of that is actually true? Social life,
including social media, is thickly populated with what
Ralph Waldo Emerson called "little statesmen and philosophers and divines"; these are know-better voices
who want to sanction your right to claim what you want
or to search as you wish. This is one reason why silence

is powerful. How does a peer know what is good for you—especially when most peer ideas seem to come out of books of quotations or untested wisdom? Choose hard experience instead.

I realize I am being absolute but I take seriously the issue of not living based on the decisions of another person. Such decisions are often the result of cultural repetition rather than recognition of *who you are.*

At the risk of sounding bellicose, I am likewise suspicious of most talk about "meaning" and "gratitude" today. Not that I reject such ideals—when they are authentic. Rather, I reject such concepts when we use them as platitudes, recitations, or excuses. In short, when we use them to conceal what we or another justly wants. In summer 2020, I was interviewed about the "gratitude movement" by an English-language newspaper, the *Deccan Herald,* based in Bangalore, India. The reporter asked, "Does gratitude mean avoidance of some real issues we have? Does it stop us from critical thinking or questioning an unjust system?" I replied:

> I think gratitude is helpful in its proper place. To me, healthful gratitude allows us to realize how fortunate we are apropos of people who truly must struggle for life. So many people in the world are denied basic necessities. For a physically secure person not to feel gratitude betrays a lack of realism.

She further asked: "Is gratitude really the key to mental peace?" Here I said: "Personally—and I realize this may be controversial and even misunderstood—I think victory and power are more important to mental peace than anything else."

*Victory and power are more important to mental peace than anything else.* I am at once comfortable and uncomfortable relaying those words. I am comfortable because they are blunt and, I believe, true. I am uncomfortable because they are easily open to misunderstanding.

We are trained to believe that the terms I used, victory and power, are corrupt, amoral, and even malevolent. But in terms of the human psyche, I contend that there is no good and evil. There is empathy and spite. The only malevolence arises from where you fall on that scale. (I revisit this theme more fully on Day 19.) Everyone reading these words knows people who profess to love the world, who claim titles like Christian, Buddhist, or progressive, yet who dwell near the polarity of spite. Wishes for power and success do not erode or otherwise determine, for good or ill, your quality of conduct, any more than claims of virtue ensure it. Indeed, when you acknowledge your wishes in a pensive and self-aware manner you do justice to honesty and, I believe, enhance your ability to see through your wishes in life. Hence, I repeat the question: *What do you want in life?*

Write down what you want. Reduce it to a simple, plain sentence. Your sentence, which I sometimes call your Definite Chief Aim or DCA in tribute to Napoleon Hill needn't encompass literally *everything* you wish for. We all want health and happiness for ourselves and those we love. We all want comfortable shelter. We want surroundings of relative peace. We want intimacy. Rather, I ask you to write down that one overarching, non-negotiable *thing*; that one core aim that you desire like breath itself. Search yourself. It is there.

As alluded earlier, you may or may not be able to attain that thing. Or you may be able to attain it but not on your terms or within your mind's-eye picture. That must be expected to some degree. The breakthrough today, however, is in *acknowledging* the thing you want, without external or internalized peer pressure.

I told this to graphic artist Josh Romero in a summer 2020 interview:

> I am in a very heavy state of mind right now where I'm fed up with orthodoxy of any kind—and there's so much of it within both the mainstream and alternative spiritual world. We always think orthodoxy comes from "those other guys" but the truth is you encounter it all over social media from people who are supposed to be on a spiritual search. For example, someone will write you can only "know God" if

you do this or that; or other times people will place labels on things, calling something "materialistic" or too "outwardly focused" or superficial or some such. I have a real problem with that because I feel that that kind of approach *takes people's questions from them* and places limits on people. I believe that sensitive men and women are capable of coming to terms with what they want in life without mediation. I don't like seeing someone's question being taken from them. If someone says, "I just want to be happy" there's always some divine who will tell them, "what do you mean by happiness?"— and I don't like that line of engagement. I think that a person knows full well what he or she means by happiness. That person could teach me something about what he or she means by happiness. I think a 12-year-old knows what he or she means by happiness. Obviously there are people among us who might be more finely attuned to their emotions than others; there might be people who more closely match my personal style and I might have more affinity with that person. But I think that we all must stop and take seriously that the individual knows something about what he or she wants. I don't like any kind of orthodoxy that takes that away from somebody, myself included.

Consider what these words mean to you today—and ask yourself with complete freshness, privacy, and lack of embarrassment: *what do I want?* Knowing does not mean receiving *but receiving of some kind will occur.* Be keenly aware of what you invite in or deflect.

# DAY 9
# UNDERSTAND POWER

I n a sense, this entire book is about the ethical attainment of power. I contend that most of what you experience as emotional anguish is the frustration of your exercise of personal power. Power is the means to see through your intentions. My definition of power involves ethical reciprocity without which power becomes force. Power without ethics is easily abused and ultimately unrenewable.

Since I am dealing with power in a literal and whole manner—we live in a world of currency, material, and relationships as much as a world of things unseen—I believe we must be unflinchingly practical about the matter if we strive for realism. Most people who talk about power in spiritual settings have none and never will. They are not artists, warriors, merchants, or farmers—so where does their power come from? God or the Higher, they may say. That may be ultimately true but wake them at 4 a.m. to say there's an emergency and see how powerful they seem. See whether they rush to help others. See how practical their resources are. Having spent time in many spiritual communities I can reasonably testify: you will probably not be reassured.

I admire Ralph Waldo Emerson's 1860 essay "Power" in which he essentially defines this elusive force in three ways. The prerequisite to power is health, Emerson writes; if someone is physically unwell all of his or her energies must go towards recovery. The remaining ingredients to power, he writes, are *concentration* and *drilling*. Concentration means absolute focus on a single aim. Without a laser-sharp focus in life, we disperse our energies and often harbor conflicting goals. (Hence, the importance of asking *what you want* yesterday.) Drilling means constant training, practice, or rehearsal. Drilling is attainment of great skill or mastery at whatever you are striving toward and requires absolute dedication. You cannot properly drill without a singular area of focus. Both qualities, concentration and drilling, work in tandem.

I believe in that formula. But in the rough-and-tumble of life it gets easily compromised. We also require the cooperation of others to accomplish our ends in life. Our colleagues may be financial backers, business partners, editors, creative collaborators, agents, and others who can help with vital tasks that are beyond one person's purview. You also need friends and intimate partners without whom life is an agonizing loneliness. Friends and intimates also pull us in new directions, without which self-expression grows stale.

One of the most frustrating experiences in life is the periodic inability to attract good colleagues, intimates, and comrades. You may be the greatest martial artist in the world, but you must have a school in which to train; you must eventually find your own students (teaching is symbiotic). Your excellence ought to attract these things . . . *ought to*. But there will be periods of frustration and fallowness. You may also, due to issues of anger or other destructive emotions, alienate people or surroundings that you need. Or you may misplace your trust finding yourself saddled with do-nothings or troublemakers. At such times, power seems very distant.

Coming to terms with power also means coming to terms with some tough truths about resources and money. We may want to push away these truths—I often do—but they are part of navigating life. Our intent is a *wholly honest* reckoning of power in the world as it is, not as we wish it to be. In essence, your success-ful transactions come down to *the ability to give others what they want in exchange for what you do*. This often means offering the following factors or currencies in this order: 1) money, 2) sex/intimacy, 3) safety, and 4) prestige/social acceptance. That is our world, most of the time. If you're a freelancer or contractor, try get-ting a client or customer to pay you, or to pay out on time, without your being able to offer one or more of those tools of exchange. And the slope of those priori-ties descends quickly in importance.

I have observed more people accommodate them-selves to others for the first factor, *money*, than any other reason. When I was younger, I naïvely believed that people *wanted* to perfect their output and abili-ties, whether in writing, presenting, editing, financial planning, or some other craft, and that their striving for excellence would gravitationally draw them towards right training, action, behavior, and company. I was wrong. In workplaces, academia, the military, and other environments, the majority of people gravitate toward whomever signs off on their vacation slips. This is a near-absolute truth that I neither like sharing nor writ-ing. Hence, if you want to wield power in this world, you must control *resources*.

I have, on occasion, made appeals to people who I felt were sketchy or who I disliked because they had the ability to commission a project. In making such appeals, I have felt almost queasy. I try my damnedest never to do this today. I will return to this point, because approaching the wrong people can create a deficit in matters of power. Our aim is to help ameliorate that deficit.

The second most powerful factor is *sexuality*. People often ask why influential or accomplished men (and mostly it is men) destroy life and livelihood in the pursuit, sometimes exploitatively, of intimacy and sex. Sexuality is the urge of perpetuation even when it is not procreative in nature, which most often it is not. Sex is, perhaps, the most overwhelmingly powerful human drive—arguably more powerful than money, since many otherwise shrewd people squander money and position to indulge it. Other people use sexuality, sometimes not always engaging in physicality, to win attention, media prominence, favors, position, money, and advancement. Another fact of worldly life.

The third factor of *safety* often comes into play when we seek an ally, champion, or protector—or are made to feel afraid. Bosses often use fear or its alleviation to manipulate. Employers or investors sometimes pit people against one another, creating an atmosphere of contest, which is ultimately fear-based. I once knew a publishing executive who routinely debased and humiliated employees as a means of motivation and for her own emotional release. In a typical display during a densely packed meeting she mentioned that the books published by an editor seated nearby often got good reviews. She paused and then added sardonically, "They don't sell but they get good reviews." I could see him silently struggle under the diminishing blow. This same boss was a grandmother. I cannot fathom anything of value she had to impart. In her indirect defense, it is not easy to find impeccable and foresightful employees; the boss can sometimes feel that he or she is funding fecklessness by the hour. In any case, the form of power that I just described is that which I most disdain. It can also end abruptly, as we will see.

Finally, there is the question of *prestige*. This is not only a matter of social status but of fashion, appearance, and self-image. People perennially gravitate toward the proverbial cool kids' lunch table. It is a constant of human psychology that we are drawn toward whoever we believe redresses the deficiency we felt in youth, which we endeavor to conceal or compensate for in adulthood. Hence, many men gravitate toward "tough guy" actors or athletes. Men and women alike seek the company of someone sexually magnetic not always because of hoped-for intimacy but because they believe that person provides them with the reflected light of charisma or sex appeal as the sun's rays bounce off the moon. I have even seen canny people choose business collaborators that way. It is a rarely spoken truth of human nature that *people gravitate toward you to fill their self-perceived deficits.*

Given what I just described, it is rarely wise to behave in an overly solicitous manner. People are not attracted to what they are or perceive themselves to be but to the person who they believe makes them *what they want to be.* This dynamic is not necessarily corrupt—in fact, it can be used to balance social scales or subvert more obvious forms of power. This is why the artist, rebel, model, or hipster is perennially powerful. People may deny it but they're fascinated with such figures and seek proximity to them.

I realize that I may be painting a stark view of human nature and I do so somberly. My wish is for power to arise from personal excellence alone—from the artist, warrior, merchant, or farmer—and not from more prurient or questionable factors. But today, Day 9, we must face the world as it is. But you can take succor from another truth: *Most of the factors and currencies that I have noted will naturally accrue to you, in greater or lesser degree, from honing your persona and abilities along the lines of the practices in this 30-day program.* I wrote at the outset: "This book is not specifically oriented toward money-getting, job change, finding a mate, or conventional models of success—although such things may and, in time, *should come*, if desired." As you advance you will probably find new openings before you and some improvement in your personal means of action and attainment.

Use what you attain wisely. Because it will also be taken away. Positions and power, like sexuality and mental acumen, fade or get quickly removed. Recall the publishing executive I mentioned earlier. Soon after the story I told, she came to believe that she was being placed under excessive financial pressure from a new corporate owner. Unaccustomed to being bossed around herself, she abruptly quit. She took a new job at another publishing giant. But she never again attained distinction or leadership. She was overlooked in meetings. Success is often situational, a fact that many who enjoy it fail to grasp. This executive still had money, a nice Manhattan address, and could lunch out at expense-account restaurants. (Although I've also been there and, believe me, there's only so much bread and olive oil and grilled salmon you can eat.) She became a *fading memory*. Likewise, one of her deputies, who copycatted her crude manner, was soon fired after the boss departed. (Don't overinvest in the good graces of the ruler.) Her life afterward was one of wandering and uncertainty. Hence, the toughest people around us can find their power abruptly stripped away, and at some point almost certainly will. Displaced powerholders may hang onto some money, but as a mogul once put it: "You can only sit your ass in one chair at a time." (And soon after saying that he, too, experienced a stunning fall from prominence.)

Since power will end, never misbehave when holding it. Never be the bully or manipulator. To purposefully or routinely intimidate people is, I think, begging for negative compensation, which will come whether publicly or privately.

If there is a key to wielding ethical power it is *self-development coupled to awareness*. Awareness itself is a form of power. Awareness may not always rescue you from having to solicit help from an unsavory person or accommodate an investor who you may not respect. But knowing and facing the power dynamics that are present at least gives you a greater sense of self-possession and choice. Awareness is a principle that only you control, at least when your psyche is unclouded by emotional or physical duress.

In closing I want to add one further element to what we have explored. You possess a solitary escape hatch from all stratagems of power-jockeying and game-playing. You hold a single trump card that surpasses all the ins-and-outs I have described. And that is: *telling the truth*. About yourself, about your expectations, about your abilities, and about your needs. Such a move may not always result in victory or temporal gains; it may not always gain you what you want or what you think you want. But acting with simple truth upends and cuts through artifice. It often shocks people. Use this power decisively—and thoughtfully.

# DAY 10
## MAKE THE ASK

ip-hop artist Cardi B observed that she did not start to earn real money until she made the ask. She stood up and asked for exactly what she wanted. She also had the abilities to deliver what others wanted. You will never know whether or to what extent you are valued *unless* you make the ask.

It took me many years of underpaid work in publishing to finally learn this lesson. Early one morning I did a revealing personal exercise. I was attending a conference at the Esalen Institute in Big Sur, California, in spring of 2009. It was on the brink of the publication of my first book, *Occult America*, and I was attending a private gathering of scholars, writers, and artists interested in esotericism and the surrounding literature and

scholarship. I made some lasting friendships and part-
nerships at that conference. It was a truly exciting and
productive event. At the time, however, I was dissatis-
fied with my job in publishing. I was the editor-in-chief
of a New Age division at Penguin—but in title only.
Mostly I was treated like an extra-senior editor. I was
paid like it, too. However, I had access to budget numbers; I knew what each book earned (or more often lost)
and I embarked on an exploratory exercise. I reviewed
two years of budgets and discovered that not only were
my front-list titles deep into the black individually and
in aggregate, but my publishing list was, in fact, so fully
into the black that it was supporting the entire imprint.
Everyone else's list or catalogue of titles was, for two
years' running, losing money by double-percentage
points. My titles were, for that time, robustly selling and
sustaining the shop. This was directly on the heels of
the Great Recession of 2008 during which not one of my
colleagues lost their jobs, which I view as my signature
achievement in publishing.

I felt validated—but still frozen in place. I didn't
"make the ask" for higher pay and position until early
2012. Why? I think I was afraid of being told no or of
confrontation. That was an emotionally driven mistake
on my part. When I finally made the ask, money and
title came quickly. I received much of what I wanted. My
progress eventually ended as my titles cooled. (Few edi-

tors have hot runs of more than ten years.) But making the ask placed me on much firmer footing for the future.

Today, Day 10, I want you to set a timetable to ask for something that you need. Or ask for it today. It may be money. It may be a legal settlement. It may be help with a vital task. Whatever it is: make the ask. Do so intelligently and without rashness—but be bold. Whatever your choice, you must make this ask *within the remaining 20 days of our program*. You may not get full resolution within that timeframe, but you must commence the process.

Another mistake I have made from time to time is agreeing to undertake a project before nailing down the financial terms. I wrongly assumed that the other party had a reasonable budget (or would be willing to make a reasonable payment from that budget), or that we had like minds about the work involved and its value. Whenever I do this (and I hope I'm done forever!) I learn anew that you must make the ask before delivering a yes. That can be difficult for artists or other creatives who are eager to undertake a project—and whom society makes feel guilty about accepting money.

Indeed, we live in a society that devalues culture and elective learning; our society often views art (unless it's an investment property) as napkins at a diner and not something you pay for. This is also why writers must, at a certain point in their careers, resist writing for free. In the early years of the Internet there developed a trend of writing or contributing free content in exchange for links to your book or another kind of product. That bargain became meaningless as shared links grew quantumly. The work-for-links approach has now been eclipsed by the rise of content-hosting websites like Medium, which, at least as of this writing, pays for articles according to the number of reads. It is not a universally applicable solution but it is a viable response to the needs of creators and it may prove useful in other areas of digital commerce.

I am friendly with channeler and author Paul Selig. Whatever your take on the extra-physical, Paul makes a statement that I have always found universally applicable and that I want to close on: "If you want something, you must first ask for it." He means that on several levels. Embrace that principle today.

# DAY 11
## F COLLEGE

I am writing these words in the midst of the 2020 Covid crisis with most college campuses shut down and students planning their fall semesters around online classes—and, in many cases, receiving no discount in tuition, including from A-list and immensely wealthy institutions like Harvard and Stanford.

I believe we are living in a time of great change in higher education, especially with the crisis of student debt, amplified by the economics of lockdown and the continued shockwaves it will bring. Whether you are a student, continuing-education student, guardian, or parent, I ask you to dedicate this day to seriously and bravely reconsidering where to allocate your education dollars, years, and efforts.

Some of the most inspiring and successful people I know did not attend college. They went directly into their careers, including gunsmithing, fashion design, tech, and film directing. I believe the trades are a wonderful career, including plumbing, contracting, landscaping, and hairstyling. I often tell my two adolescent sons, "You can be an electrician who loves opera, can't you?" I know someone from New England who grudgingly attended a single year of traditional college and then begged his parents to allow him to quit and enroll in a year-long program in gunsmithing in Colorado. His parents were skeptical (they wanted him to take a "safe" career path) but eventually conceded. After certification, my friend quickly rose to become one of the premier restorers of antique firearms in the nation and later the owner-operator of one of New England's most high-end firearm stores. None of his distinctive success would've been possible if mom and dad had insisted on a more traditional path, or if my friend hadn't found the gumption to pursue a career that reflected his highest passions and abilities. Maybe this is you. Or your child. Or someone you care for. I can tell you this: when you speak with a person who loves and feels a sense of command in his or her work, you feel you are in the presence of a small and self-selected elite society.

Years ago I attended a literary conference in Dallas, Texas, where I was sharing a roundtable lunch with a group of editors, writers, and agents. One literary agent told me that in her former work she had been a prison guard. (Not the response you expect when asking, "So, how'd you get into publishing?") Working as a prison guard is grueling: the pay is low (a chronic unfairness) and the work can be dangerous and draining. You may also have valid objections to the nature of our prison system. But I must note the following: the wisdom and stories that she had, her sheer insight into human nature (what she said could've appeared in an Elmore Leonard novel) had everyone leaning in as she spoke. To this day, I recall some of her psychological insights, particularly about how to forge bargains with people in harrowing conditions and how such bargains get sustained or shattered. When the conversation returned to publishing it all seemed humdrum and pedestrian. I do not mean to overly generalize or idealize: my colleague's previous work was dangerous, came with health challenges, and she had her own good reasons for moving on. But I must also say: to be outstanding in an unusual field is, in my view, far superior to being a standard member of a more conventional one.

Are college courses worth it? Yes, if certification is involved. There is no choice for an engineer or a medical professional. But in my pursuit of a BA, the only courses I found of lasting value were mathematics and a few composition and journalism classes. Those were probably the only classes that imparted skills and ideas that I draw upon today. Otherwise, I learned my craft as a writer at the student newspaper, where I put in long hours, and also as a hardworking freelancer. (I once wrote for a radical newspaper that paid 2.5 cents per word. When I complained about it, my roommate said: "Use smaller words.")

I am not saying that college is never the right course. But I urge parents and kids on this day—Day 11—to rethink their preconceptions about higher education. The costs are astronomical and the payoff is questionable unless, as noted, one is entering the professions, sciences, or receiving some kind of certification, like physical therapy. (In that vein, I am a big fan of community colleges.) I attended a nationally ranked state school in the 1980s where tuition—adjusted for inflation—would be under $1,600 a semester today. Dorms? About $955 inflation adjusted. For real. Those days are sadly gone. All told, your average private school today costs about $50,000 a year and a state school about $35,000, though less if you're a resident or commuter.

In fairness, I was an English major so maybe I am closing the door after the fact. But I do believe that greater educative purpose is served by reading the classics (for which you'll rarely find time in working life) and in honing your writing skills rather than engaging in deconstructive theory (spoon please).

Lest that sound kneejerk, I have witnessed waves of young graduates with high-priced humanities degrees stream into book publishing, where I worked for more than twenty-five years, with boundless opinions but scant and sketchy work habits. The pay in publishing is notoriously low, which is also why most publishing houses are overpopulated by not-hugely-intrepid sons and daughters of privilege. Sorry, but it must be said.

College is supposed to help you grow and expand your boundaries. I believe that discipline and rigor give a person the foundation for experiment and growth. Experiment as an end to itself leads to idolizing experiment.

I'm skeptical of higher degrees, as well. At one point in my publishing career I considered taking business classes or enrolling in a continuing education program to earn an MBA. Thankfully, I was dissuaded by educator and author Ronald Gross, who is responsible for popularizing the term "lifelong learning." Ron convinced me that I could learn just as much on the job by throwing myself into the financial details of my work and collaborating with business managers, which would prove both educative and career advancing, and also save a lot of money. Ron was correct on every count.

Imagine the liberation of not taking on reams of debt, meeting tough repayment schedules, and paying for the myriad college "extras" that the budgeting tables often omit. Sit down today and map out on paper or spreadsheet, however roughly, the projected costs along with projected alternatives, for yourself or another. Take this day to think freely, flexibly, and bravely about what an education really means in the twenty-first century. It could benefit you or a loved one for decades to come.

# DAY 12

## FIND THE SCISSORS YOURSELF

T oday is about cultivating self-sufficiency. In his 1841 lecture "Man the Reformer," Ralph Waldo Emerson asked: "Can we not learn the lesson of self-help? Society is full of infirm people, who incessantly summon others to serve them."

Emerson was not referring to the destitute, but rather to those who clamor for life's luxuries even while producing little themselves. By contrast, Emerson asked: "Can anything be so elegant as to have few wants and to serve them one's self, so as to have somewhat left to give, instead of being always prompt to grab?"

Pursuing this ideal of "self-help"—Emerson actually coined the term in his lecture—does not require a personal crisis, addiction, or the heralding of some thunderous change in your life. In can begin, and in some regards must begin, in subtle and quietly self-determined ways. I believe that lasting changing often begins with the smallest and steadiest of steps. Today we begin that change—and it starts with the pursuit of domestic and workplace self-sufficiency.

I am a great admirer of a twentieth-century spiritual teacher named Vernon Howard (1918–1992). I never met Vernon but this book is influenced by his outlook and directness. Vernon made the observation that we automatically, and often by default, burden others with our needs, creating a cycle of unnecessary dependency that expands throughout our lives in matters small and large. This cycle also fosters resentment in others even if they never let on. To break this cycle, Vernon said, start by doing small things for yourself. For example, when you are at home instead of burdening someone else with a question about where a household object can be located—such as tape or scissors—take it upon yourself to fully search for the object, which can almost always be found. Only if a search has failed to turn it up should you ask another, "Do you know where the scissors are?" You will be amazed at how rarely you even need to ask for help from another person, and thus place a needless claim on his or her time, if you take just one step further than you're accustomed. Make it a practice.

Do you want to carry your own load through life or rely upon others to carry it? Do not respond too quickly to that question. I've made huge mistakes in life because I liked the idea—however much I concealed it from myself at the time—of making *someone else responsible for carrying my load* in one way or another. We all do this. But overly depending on others erodes your sense of self-respect as it also erodes your basic abilities and acumen. Starting today, make the effort to do as much for yourself as possible in small situations and you will see how this reverberates through larger and more consequential areas of life.

This does not mean that you will not need to ask for help. But the ask should occur only after you've made every reasonable effort to unclog a toilet, locate a tool, install or remove an air conditioner, plaster a crack, or mount a picture. Even if you do so imperfectly (and you ought to see my sewing) you will have won a victory. And you will sense it. So will others, even if indirectly or subtly. In time, such actions will improve your relationships and enhance your self-respect.

Years ago I volunteered to perform ten days of trail maintenance on the Appalachian Mountains in New York State. The other volunteers and I dug drainage channels, blazed trees, cleared brush and branches, and set or reset natural boundaries. It was grueling labor in the mid-summer heat. I loved every minute of it and never slept better. About halfway through the experience, however, one of the younger volunteers grew desultory. She began asking others—at mealtime, on the trail, during labor—to find things for her, hand things to her, and perform small tasks that were easily within her reach. Resentment began to simmer at her somewhat entitled attitude. This occurs all the time in life: again, people rarely express it, but this dynamic contributes to below-the-surface resentment that prevails in many households and workplaces. The cycle can be easily broken by displaying self-sufficiency in small ways.

Vow today: *I will first make every effort to meet my own needs before requesting assistance from another; I will enlist another's help only when matters of personal wellbeing or safety are involved or I have made every reasonable effort on my own.*

Can a small change be revolutionary? Today we find out.

# DAY 13
## GIVE UP ONE THING THAT CAUSES YOU PAIN

We remain attached to unproductive situations because of fear. We are often more frightened of losing a theorized or imagined benefit than we are desirous of freeing ourselves. Today's task is to rid yourself of *one thing*—such as a relationship, social commitment, personal practice, or client—that causes you pain.

There are no set parameters on the seeming largeness or smallness of the tie that is cut. The only requirement is that it be something empirically real—and not, for example, "negative thoughts" or other vagaries of the psyche from which none of us will ever wholly be free. Once you have selected the practice, place, person, or thing that you wish to get rid of, do so quietly and without public signaling (which keeps others from shaking your resolve) and determine to effectively burn the bridge behind you.

What you do one time you can do again. One of the key points of this book is that the micro and the macro are interconnected and, ultimately, the same. Hence, any deliberate act that you take, while significant on its own terms, fortifies and expands your ability to take similar approaches on larger scales.

My personal decision was to give up Facebook. Facebook has been a wonderful tool for me in many ways. I've met lots of great people there. It has been an important tool for me to expose people to my books and events. It has a promotional dimension. But I had to let it go. Facebook feeds too much that I consider unproductive in human relations. Something about the tech of Facebook—I cannot quite place my finger on it—fosters a frivolity of comment and an excess of familiarity with strangers or near-strangers. I am writing this not as a tech whiz, who would surely have different insights, but as a user, which in some ways may be more valuable.

On Facebook, I encountered countless episodes of people commenting on articles that they hadn't read—literally—or complaining over secondary issues, like politics, which may be only tangentially related to a given post. This included board members of spiritual groups as well as random passersby. Naturally, I realize that the problem of social media and blather is by no means unique to Facebook and occurs endlessly on Twitter, Instagram, and elsewhere. But there is something about those two social media outlets that requires people to say a thing before the social media "world" as it were. On Facebook, however, there is a kind of *manufactured intimacy*. Facebook's tech creates a sense of inter-personalism and familiarity which tends to perpetuate (just as its algorithm prioritizes) confrontative posts.

I once posted something about positive thinking, a philosophy of which I am a longtime advocate and critic. A reasonably well-known spiritual writer complained that I was neglecting the dark side of positive thinking. As an example, he posted a link to a book that he felt supplied a corrective critique, saying that I seemed "unaware" of its author's point of view. I replied that not only have I written critically of positive-mind metaphysics for years but, in fact, the book that he recommended was one that I had commissioned, titled, and published—my name is all over the inside. I exited the chain. But I noticed that the chain went on and on and on. It's probably still going on. This is the frivolity over which I left Facebook. It's not just a matter of petty arguments, which are omnipresent. Rather, it is—how can I put it?—this frumpy, fuddy-duddy, loudmouth-

Uncle-Ralph-at-Thanksgiving quality that permeates many discussions.

Maybe it's demographics. I do not know. But the culture is plain. No sooner do you post a mild dissent to some shopworn spiritual idea than someone responds with a fortune-cookie expression or a piece of orthodoxy. It's not all political. But it relates to why politics are what they are on Facebook.

I believe that part of the dynamic I am describing is based on the limit of 5,000 "friends" per page. Before leaving I switched to a public page. But I didn't personally like the tech, which seemed like a friend page but for a product. For a little while I retained my pages but with few new posts. Yet as I distanced myself from Facebook in favor of other media, I began to feel as though I was maintaining an unkempt room somewhere or an unvisited property, which I was allowing to fall into disuse and disrepair.

I began viewing Facebook as more hindrance than help. I wanted it cleanly gone.

Now, I obviously have an interest in reaching out to readers, but I felt that if I am going to stand behind this step I must act on it in a manner that places my skin in the game. So, on Thursday, July 30, 2020, contemporaneous with my writing this section, I deleted my account. It felt good, as though I had unloaded an old clunker that no longer suited me.

This sacrifice, while it certainly carried weight in my life, is fairly benign in terms of emotional stakes. (Though I would be less-than-forthcoming if I did not acknowledge the time and emotions I invested in occasional bickering on Facebook, a fact I am not proud of—and also happy to be done with.) There are, of course, tougher and more intimate ties to cut. And I ask you to select one today. Your choice can be profoundly daring—and freeing.

Part of my inspiration for this section was a July 2020 article posted by illustrator and writer August Lamm, "The Case for Giving Up." Lamm wrote in incredibly stark and honest terms about how a spinal disability caused her increasing physical pain when drawing. She finally decided to give it up: she decided to draw no longer. It was a profoundly intimate decision made largely without the support or understanding of her peers. Every time Lamm had previously sought to quit, her determination got undermined by a chorus of unsolicited cheerleaders.

"The truth," Lamm wrote, "was sidelined by relentless optimism, and I began to see my pain as something to be downplayed or outright ignored. I entered into a silent pact with myself: I agreed to carry on drawing until my loved ones agreed that it was time for me to step away. Only with their permission would I be released."

Lamm finally realized that she could not dote on the approbation of others:

I believed that if I could just convince people that my disability was legitimate, they would let me walk away from my career guilt-free. I wanted them to tell me that I needed to stop, that I had no other choice, that it was incredible how long I'd carried on but that no amount of money or attention could balance out the harm I was doing to my body.

This is not what they told me. Instead, they told me that I would succeed regardless. They told me stories of broken bodies healed through veganism, mushrooms, yoga. They told me to cut out dairy, or to drink raw milk every day. They told me to watch a documentary about someone with the exact same condition who'd started a gratitude practice and gone on to paint the ceiling of the Sistine Chapel. Or something. If only they could remember the name of it. They had no doubt it would change my life.

They told me a lot of conflicting things, but there was one thing they could all agree on: no matter what happens, you should never give up. Giving up is anti-American! Giving up is for losers, weaklings, sad-sacks. Giving up is the stuff of nightmares, cautionary tales, and before-photos. No one wants to hear about it—you certainly won't find it in the self-help section or on daytime TV. Giving up is the ultimate failure of willpower. It is a fatal blow, and it is a blow you inflict upon yourself. But what do you do if it's your only option?

I couldn't wait any longer. I left without a word, disabling my Instagram and resolving to stay offline for at least a month. I called friends and family to explain what had happened. Their response was unanimous: "I had no idea it was that bad." I was stunned. These were the people who'd watched me do physical therapy, take pain pills, and draw uncomfortably at an adaptive easel. These were the people who'd listened to me cry into my cellphone from across the Atlantic, inconsolable because I'd flown all the way to Paris just to hide out in my rental flat, crying hot rivers down swollen cheeks, holding my neck protectively in my hand as though the vertebrae might break apart and scatter across the floor like beads? Would the pain never resonate with them the way the perseverance had?

Seen from a certain perspective, I, too, have been part of our culture's huzzah choir. But consistency is no virtue when it blinds us to a person's true needs. Consider how *unseen* Lamm felt by the very people eager to tell her "chin up." Is that empathy? Are more doses of encouragement *always* the answer? William Blake wrote in *The Marriage of Heaven and Hell*: "One Law for the Lion & Ox is Oppression."

Lamm's action and her description of it are a brilliant assertion of individual need over majority bromides. Her testimony also suggests why you must not always share or vet your intentions with your peer group. You must sometimes act unilaterally. This is the kind of bravery I want you to bring to the task of giving up something that causes you pain. What you release may not be as foundational as what Lamm describes. But I want you to get the feeling of *what is possible*. It will grow from there. The first step is wholly and intimately your own.

# DAY 14
# ACKNOWLEDGE THAT YOU DO NOT KNOW

**W**e often poison our relationships, as well as the overall social, intellectual, and political culture, by assuming that we know things we do not. We often speak from prejudice and self-certainty—and with the untested conviction that our informational intake provides us with a fullness of perspective on a person, issue, or incident.

Today I want you to stop posting, speaking, or opining about things with which you have only casual or indirect experience.

This may mean not repeating a story about a friend or coworker that you have no way of verifying or knowing that person's side of. This means avoiding making sweeping generalizations about a political issue that you may know about only from tweets or cherry-picked news and opinion blogs. It means not discussing or commenting on the work of writers you haven't actually read or done more than read coverage about. (Haven't read Jordan Petersen, Angela Davis, or Ayn Rand? Don't discuss them.) It means curbing your use of adjectives about topics, people, or controversies that are distant or peripheral to you. These kinds of communication habits make us into sloppy and pedestrian thinkers, and thicken the smog of know-it-all comments in our know-nothing culture.

When you desist from idle chatter not only will the depth and gravity of what you do say improve, but you will earn greater respect and, I believe, authentically feel more at home in yourself.

I have often noted the deleterious effects of gossip. When you repeat or listen to rumors or gossip I think you enact within yourself the same debased qualities you are describing since we tend to project onto others the traits we ourselves harbor; hence we disguise and inoculate ourselves from our own cruelties and flaws in what we say about another. Gossip is displacement. I am not saying that one should desist from calling out injustice or protecting people. Rather, I am referencing gossip as distraction, tonic, entertainment and pastime. I am talking about deriving a thrill or sense of self-elevation from seeing someone else humiliated.

\* \* \*

In 2020, a serious controversy arose at *The New York Times* when the op-ed page published Arkansas Senator Tom Cotton's call to deploy federal troops to quell disorder associated with protests in American cities. About a year before that op-ed appeared, I was told by a first-hand witness that the same senator back when he was a residence-hall director at Harvard reacted very mildly and in a notably calm fashion when a drug-infused dorm party got out of hand and had to be clamped down. "Tom was so chill," my acquaintance recalled. No police or security were brought in and everything got amicably settled.

Why, I wondered, was the senator-to-be "so chill" in his own social sphere but would endorse a near-unprecedented move of dispatching troops into urban settings where they were expressly unwanted by most local authorities and residents?

Obviously the two things differ in scale. But this dichotomy highlights a general emotional pattern in human nature. Cotton felt a sense of familial ease in the social setting he knew; he was notably calm. He acted from the opposing polarity toward a setting with which he was unfamiliar. Why couldn't the "chill" dorm monitor serve as a moderating figure versus a lead-by-bayonet town crier?

We do this kind of thing all the time—and it is by no means limited to one political tendency or another. We determine that we know the facts and needs involved in key issues whereas we are *acting from emotions or prejudice*. Most of us, most of the time, desire little more than a world in which we feel personally safe. Whatever factors or associations trigger a sense of safety or its absence determine where we fall on civic and economic issues, often with little thought about larger unknowns, complexifying facts, or *the experience of other actors in the matter*. For example, generalized critiques of "woo" or "magical thinking" almost always come from cultural snobs who are no more capable of recognizing themselves as such than are anti-intellectuals who call themselves skeptics. This is the malady of human nature: certainty that my opinions, however conditioned or half-wrought, come from a place of higher perspective or realism.

The suspension of self-certainty—your task for Day 14—actually opens you to vaster streams of information and makes you a positive force for decreasing some of the smog of blather on social media and in daily life. Blather, which is to say frivolous, uninformed, or superfluous opining, is nothing new and will always be with us; but social media has amplified it to levels that humanity has never before experienced. We must depollute.

*   *   *

We are all generalists by necessity. I cannot know the facts behind most social policies, much less the intimacies of other people's lives. Hence, I reply upon sources that I trust. We all do. It is necessary. But reliance upon a subset of trusted authorities, while sometimes valid, can, particularly in matters that go beyond personal wellbeing, foment a groupthink mentality in which everything that your trusted sources say is considered right while rejected sources are greeted with eyerolling. PR maestro Edward Bernays wrote in his 1923 book *Crystalizing Public Opinion*: "Man is never so much at home as when he is on the bandwagon." What's more, Bernays noted, the individual is most heedful of voices that he or she identifies as part of the same "buffalo herd."

I have no solution to this problem. But I promise that if you enact the principle of self-uncertainty as a mental habit you will not only come to know more (not knowing *is* knowing something) but you will also shine a light to others and improve the anger-infested atmosphere of opinion. None of this means that you do not express a point of view. It means, rather, that your point of view be expressed less often, more substantially, and—above all—with awareness that some facts are necessarily elusive or missing.

Uncertainty in matters beyond your personal purview is a mark of refinement. Uncertainty does not foster inaction but rather action with greater weight. Only fools are certain absent experience. Knowing that you do not know is powerful.

# DAY 15
## RECONSIDER FORGIVENESS

The title of this segment is not intended ironically or as a rhetorical bait-and-switch. Today I ask you to seriously reconsider the hallowed spiritual principle of forgiveness. This is not to provoke but to urge you to determine for yourself—not based on what someone else has decided, either in antiquity or modernity—whether such a principle consistently serves your needs, ethics, aspiration, and outlook.

To be sure, virtually every religious tradition that has reached us, as well as every new religious movement, affirms the necessity of forgiveness. Turning the other cheek and forgiving the transgressor are at the heart of Christianity. This principle is less pronounced but still deep seated in Judaism. Forgiveness resonates, albeit with different rationales, in Vedic traditions. To forgive is at the center of modern spiritual programs like the Twelve Steps and *A Course in Miracles*.

Friends whom I consider brilliant have argued to me, with persuasiveness, that without forgiveness history could not march forward: Jews could never forgive Germans, Armenians could never forgive Turks, Japanese could never forgive Americans. My friend Richard Smoley writes with sterling precision in his book *The Deal* that forgiveness is the one escape hatch we are given from our own karma—and that we will soon enough require the same forgiveness we offer another.

I have worked intently with forgiveness for seven years prior to this writing. I have prayed, pondered, assayed, and studied. I reject the moral imperative of forgiveness. I invite you on this day, Day 15, to join me in this reconsideration—not to echo it but to test it.

Personally speaking, I believe that the moral suasion to forgive often places the individual in an unnatural position and produces inner division that gets diverted into other, often hostile or self-negating behaviors. This day is your opportunity to decide, *on your own terms*, whether the injunction to forgive has in a particular case served your needs, or perhaps impeded your sense of closure and rightness.

What I write here does not mean that forgiveness is unwarranted in given situations. Nor that it has not healed wounds. It means only that I reject forgiveness as a blanket rule, spiritual imperative, or ethical necessity. And today we free ourselves from unquestioned fealty to forgiveness.

Am I arguing for revenge? Not necessarily. Rather, I am arguing that a finer, more realistic, and nobler principle than forgiveness appears in *abiding*. In enduring hurt, suffering, wounding, or trespass with the realism that life is reciprocal, suffering is inevitable—and the vow that another person's trespass is wind at your back for the progress toward what you must be and do in life. Have you been defeated? Consider the words of the temporary victor Lady Macbeth: "'Tis safer to be that which we destroy / Than by destruction dwell in doubtful joy."

I take a spiritual view of life. By spiritual I mean extra-physical. As I have noted in *The Miracle Club* and elsewhere, we have amassed sufficient evidence, not only from the testimony of seekers, but from studies in psychical research, relativity, quantum theory, and neuroplasticity among others to conclude that materialism—the belief that matter alone reproduces itself—is insufficient to cover all the bases of life. Thoughts impact neural pathways. Anomalous transfer of information, or ESP, is statistically settled. Time bends based on velocity and gravity. Sentient observation effectively determines the locality of subatomic particles. In short, thought is a force. This is true inasmuch as gravity is a force. We can debate terms, conditions, and consistency but gravity exists: mass is attracted to itself. Likewise we participate in detectable extra-physical and nonlinear modes of existence. Hence, to speak of reciprocity (which I prefer to karma) is more than metaphor. What I visit upon another person I ultimately, or in a more immediate fashion, visit upon myself due to our common metaphysics.

I believe that a better—by which I mean realer—response to pain is to use it as a goad to development. This, I believe, is what nature intended. William Blake wrote in *The Marriage of Heaven and Hell*: "Opposition is true Friendship." Starting this day work with that statement for six months. Opposition not only exposes where I need fortification but spurs me to the creative powers of necessity. Without friction we would remain intellectual and emotional children. I see this as the esoteric meaning behind the expulsion from the Garden: the snake emancipated. With emancipation came suffering. And so the individual became a creative actor rather than an object. Should Adam and Eve *forgive* Yahweh for the inconceivable cruelty of condemning humanity to forever being born in sin for a single ancestral transgression? Does the parabolic "sacrifice" of his son redeem or compound that sentence? Friction is neither to be forgiven nor understood (especially when "understanding" results in ethical paralysis). Friction is our human and spiritual situation.

From time to time—though less often than you'd think—I hear from religionists telling me how I've *completely* misunderstood this or that; quoting Scripture; telling me how they are going to pray for me; how love will overcome all. Try this experiment. Next time someone presents you with one of those arguments, watch how they behave when they are told "no." That response is their philosophy. Philosophy is conduct. I am not a Christian. But in conduct I am a better Christian than most of my detractors.

Someone messaged me recently: "Hello Mitch, I enjoyed watching some of your lectures. I just want to say: infinite love will overcome evil." I replied: "Since some people consider my ideas 'evil' I am careful with statements about overcoming."

In matters of self-verification, I am deeply influenced by Ralph Waldo Emerson's 1841 essay "Self-Reliance." Cultural prejudice and the endless need for snappy digital copy are conscripting Emerson to critical mockery. There is no antidote for that. But it speaks to why you must eschew commentary for source material. Here is a passage that impacts my thinking:

> I remember an answer which when quite young I was
> prompted to make to a valued adviser, who was wont

to importune me with the dear old doctrines of the church. On my saying, What have I to do with the sacredness of traditions, if I live wholly from within? my friend suggested,—"But these impulses may be from below, not from above." I replied, "They do not seem to me to be such; but if I am the Devil's child, I will live then from the Devil." No law can be sacred to me but that of my nature.

A law, in order to be a law, must be ever-operative. I do not see forgiveness as an ethical or spiritual law. I see it as an option only. There exist other options. I've given you one. Now go and study.

# DAY 16
## ESCAPE CRUELTY

If you know my work you are aware of my views on the necessity of escaping cruel people. This step is so important that it can revolutionize your life by itself—and I would never make such a statement without deepest seriousness. Here is your vital task for today: *Cut all ties with a cruel figure in your present and immediate life.*

For all of our therapeutic language, our culture does a poor job of identifying and acting on the problem of cruelty. I am not talking about figures from the news or someone tucked away in your past. I am talking about the problem of your being psychologically abused in the here and now, front and center, by someone in close proximity: a boss, neighbor, in-law, spouse, friend (save us from our friends), partner, or coworker.

I am not interested in people's motives for abuse. All of us have our motives and difficult emotional histories. All of us have behaviors that are diagnosable in one way or another. I do not care, ultimately, whether someone is a "narcissist" or whatever term is in vogue. I care only that on this day *you escape someone who has proven him or herself a bully, serial liar, diminishing smartass, crook*— or all these things.

A bully almost always behaves with plausible denial or what is called gaslighting. You know it when it happens: someone sends a stealth missile at you, often in the form of a backhanded compliment, diminishing joke, subtle putdown, or veiled accusation. If you respond defensively (what other response is there?) you're told you're being "too sensitive" or reading too much into what was said. You are not. Hostile people *always* use some variant of that excuse. It is a manipulative trope. Neither listen to nor tolerate it.

We often complexify things that are actually very simple. Our go-along-to-get-along peer culture conditions us to accept harassment or cruelty so as not to embarrass ourselves, suffer consequences (there are *always* consequences in life), or to maintain surface civility in family or workplace settings. But cruelty should not be tolerated, explained, or treated with faux-diplomacy. Others may do so if they wish; not you.

Peers sometimes collude with the bully when telling us that we do not see reality; that we are misreading someone's innocent motives. In select cases that criticism may have value. But often it is an over-used feint that deprives you of your capacity to maturely size up a relationship or predicament.

I have little faith in the human situation but a lot of faith in the sensitive individual to determine his or her own needs and feelings of safety. Let no one take that from you.

As alluded, lot of good has come from our therapeutic culture. Self-help books, support groups, practical spirituality, and therapy sessions have granted us a vocabulary and conceptual framework to discuss our feelings and conflicts in ways that were unavailable to previous generations. But one of the negatives to emerge from therapeutic and self-help culture is the over-applied and under-examined notion that we must primarily *change ourselves* in the face of conflict or suffering. Sometimes that is true. More often self-change must serve as an adjunct to other actions. But in no case, I believe, does the principle of self-change substitute for cutting ties with a tormentor or cruel aggressor, including those who behave subtly.

I have seen innocent people, including adolescents and young adults, suffer prolonged disrespect or humiliation simply because they were made to feel helpless, physically and psychologically, to separate from a hostile actor. Outright separation was something that no spiritual guide, therapist, adviser, or teacher had suggested or validated; yet more often than you think you *can* remove yourself from a brutish or manipulative figure and burn your bridges behind you. Consequences be damned. Nor, I believe, should you be deterred by anyone who excuses or covers for cruelty.

I once worked in an office where one figure who probably suffered from what could be called a borderline personality disorder continually tormented her colleagues. Over the course of several years different employees of varying temperaments were made to feel afraid and harassed. They complained to the boss who constantly deflected their concerns telling them it was just a "personality conflict" and the parties had to work things out themselves. That was, in my view, a compound injury (if not a prurient enjoyment of seeing other people kicked around). The innocent parties needed relief. Some of them actually quit in order to get it.

Now, I am not suggesting that you can always quit your job, switch your school, or leave your home because you are mistreated. I wish that you could; but in some cases we face consequences that are simply too grave or we lack mobility. You may have urgent economic needs, which, for the time being, necessitate proximity to a cruel person. In such cases, what should you do? First be starkly honest with yourself: are you truly bound and not just using that notion as an excuse for inaction? Fear of change is not a valid reason to remain in proximity to cruelty. As alluded, there are *always* consequences in life—whether we are active or inert—and that fact alone does not support accommodating cruelty.

You signed up for this 30-day program and every step is vital. There is no room for hiding. If, however, upon searching your psyche and circumstances you find that you are truly bound to that person for implacable reasons of commerce, shelter, or sustenance, then I offer the following approach. Acknowledge to yourself—and yourself alone—that person's cruelty; admit how truly harmful his or her behavior is, how grotesquely inappropriate it is, and make no excuses for it. Again, everything has a diagnostic code; that does not lighten or excuse mistreatment. Next, vow to separate from that person for the present as an *internal fact*—tell yourself with total conviction that his or her goading, barbs, tricks, or threats mean nothing to you internally and will garner no agreement or response. You are free. Announce that to yourself. Mean it! Finally, and most importantly, *vow to separate as a physical fact at the first possible opportunity*. That opportunity will come. Your conviction is step one in its arrival.

And one critical point: *never* tell or let on to the cruel person what you are doing. Telling that person will only invite his or her scorn and manipulation and thus weaken your resolve.

Also, when you separate from someone physically, whether it comes immediately or in time, neither trumpet nor broadcast it. Proceed decisively but quietly. Tell no one unless it is necessary. As regards the person himself, if you have no plans to see a hostile actor do not make plans. Let the relationship wither of its own accord. Say nothing to him or her unless it is required. If you must formally cut ties, such as in a relationship with a significant other or a client, then do so as plainly as possible. And just step away. Be firm but nondramatic. The point is not to invite criticism or judgment—you've had enough of both—but to remove cruelty from your life as a psychological and physical bond.

You have no idea how much you stand to gain. Once you move away from a cruel person you will rediscover traits in yourself—confidence, humor, physical grace, evenhandedness—that you had almost forgotten you possessed. The wrong settings and company deprive us of these qualities. Take them back by revoking your consent to cruelty. I am not suggesting that proximity to the wrong company is the only thing that ails us. Inner work remains vital. But our spiritual and therapeutic imperatives have inadvertently undermined an equal truth: life is relationship and overt or subtle torment has no place in that scheme.

# WRITE A BIO

Who are you? I do not mean that question in some ponderous or stripped-down, existential fashion. You are a thinking, feeling being who has worked, loved, sacrificed, and experienced successes and failures. You are educated, either by degree, by life, or both. You have vital work that you must pursue in the world, whether for pay today or promise to come.

Taking stock of this, I want you on this day to write a short and publicly usable bio. One that lets people know who you are, both personally and professionally. If called upon, you should be at the ready to use this brief bio in any and all circumstances. It should be what you'd like to see appear on Wikipedia, in a catalogue, or on a webpage.

I take this exercise seriously on several levels. First, it prioritizes your work in the world, which I do not see as a misplaced priority. In fact, most of our lives are work and relationships. That is why I tell people that they should never be embarrassed to acknowledge their own wishes or questions about money, jobs, romance, and so forth. When I occasionally do Tarot card readings (which I was doing free for healthcare workers at the outset of the Covid crisis) the vast majority of questions I receive are about love and career. People are sometimes embarrassed by this. They announce their queries in tones of near-apology. I always tell them that they should not be sheepish about having leading concerns about career and romance. Those areas, or what follows from them, make up about 90 percent of your life. Talk of "meaning" may sound pretty; but actual meaning is how we spend our daily hours.

When I initially wrote a professional bio for my first website (known as "the clunker") around 2004, I was stymied. I didn't want to sound egotistical or like a showboat, so I played it too conservatively. I described myself as a writer and editor but with no highlighting of what really mattered to me or who I was. A teacher told me, "You need more of yourself in this." He crafted a sentence for me that I used for a long time: "Mitch Horowitz is a writer and publisher of many years' experience with a lifelong interest in man's search for meaning." The latter phrase is a reference to Viktor Frankl's *Man's Search for Meaning*, a book that was central to my early search. Although I haven't used that description for years—the terminology no longer speaks to me in the same way— the line still shows up sometimes online or in event listings, and I am fine with that. Today, however, I use a different opening, which begins the author bio that you'll find at the end of this book: "Mitch Horowitz is a historian of alternative spirituality and one of today's most literate voices of esoterica, mysticism, and the occult."

For a second sentence, I selected a line that my significant other, filmmaker Jacqueline Castel, wrote as part of a joint project; I felt so understood by her words that I asked if I could adopt it: "Mitch illuminates outsider history, explains its relevance to contemporary life, and reveals the longstanding quest to bring empowerment and agency to the human condition." I could never have written that sentence myself. I didn't see that in my work in quite that way until someone else did. Again, some aspect of ego—or fear of it—often blinds us to the keynotes of our lives.

\*     \*     \*

Notice that the biographical lines above (you can read the full result in the "about the author" at the end of this book) make relatively little reference to actual professional roles or achievements, at least in the strictest sense. Rather, those opening lines depict what I try to accomplish in broad strokes, providing a sense of the individual rather than relying on institutional or scholarly affiliations. Although I later do make such references, I believe the opening sentences capture what my friend was driving me towards earlier with his references to a "search for meaning."

Now it's your turn. Today, Day 17, I want you to create a short bio that tells the world who you really are. It should be two to three paragraphs. My bio at the end of this book is longer, but it is also written in such a way that it can be easily shortened, cut off at any point like a wire news story, and it often appears that way.

You may not complete this short bio in one day since these kinds of endeavors benefit from (and almost always require) revision and refinement, sometimes over a considerable stretch of time. But you must begin. You must produce a serviceable draft. And you will, of course, periodically want to alter your bio to reflect new achievements, life changes, or priorities. As noted, it is often difficult to see ourselves, so you will probably need the help of a trusted friend, partner, or teacher in writing your bio. This is one of the few exercises in this book that is collaborative.

In that vein, before I arrived at the opening line above, I showed my bio, then posted on my website, to an acquaintance who said: "I feel like I am looking at a wall of text. I want to get to the heart of who you are—what is your story?"

That prompted me to return to the challenge I was first issued in 2004. I knew it was time for a thorough revisitation of my professional self-description. Indeed, it was as though a light went on: the more conventional opening lines I had been using (about being a PEN Award-winning historian, the author of this-and-that, and so on) gave way to a broader and more meaningful statement. So, once again, do not worry about the need to revise your bio—sometimes across several years. You will almost certainly need to periodically revise it. The point is to start. Today.

As you've probably surmised, this is not purely an exercise in personal self-definition but also in announcing yourself and your activities to the world. The aim is to capture who you are in a way that is not only sincere and self-revealing but also highlights your persona to others. All of us are required from time to time to provide a bio: for an event, job or school application, conference, or social-media page. Indeed, being *seen* is a vital part of life. Never underestimate how important that is.

Consider this short letter that philosopher William James (1842–1910) wrote on April 6, 1896, to his students at Radcliffe College in Cambridge, Massachusetts, after they sent him the gift of a potted azalea tree for Easter. James was already a world-known psychologist when he sent this note. The emphasis is my own:

> Dear Young Ladies, I am deeply touched by your remembrance. It is the first time anyone ever treated me so kindly, so you may well believe that the impression on the heart of the lonely sufferer will be even more durable than the impression on your minds of all the teachings of Philosophy 2A. *I now perceive one immense omission in my Psychology, the deepest principle of Human Nature is the craving to be appreciated, and I left it out altogether from the book, because I had never had it gratified till now.*

Many people in your sphere, regardless of the habit of googling other people, do not actually know, see, or appreciate your strivings, work, and accomplishments. *Share them.*

A bio should also be personal without being mawkishly self-disclosing. Let me know who you are, where you come from, have journeyed to, and what you are doing today. Certain things are private and must remain so. But your personhood, as actually lived, is one whole. A short bio should make it clear exactly who you are dealing with: your achievements, experience, efforts, perspective. Also—and this is a key point—your bio ought to be structured in such a way that it can be repurposed and used for nearly any occasion, whether those noted above or a press release, investor document, social-media post, or professional engagement.

Be flexible in how you approach this task. The content and emphases are yours alone. Don't be too formulaic. Eschew a cookie-cutter approach. But strive nonetheless to produce a sturdy and refined document—even if it takes some time—which announces you to the world and is usable in different settings. If it's helpful, use mine at the end as a guideline—or select another "about the author" by someone you admire. Once you have a decent version of that document, you will possess more than a brief bio: you will possess a better idea of yourself and, hence, others will have a better idea of you, too. Honor the principle of appreciation. Tell the world who you are.

# DAY 18
## WIN NOBLY

**E**arlier I wrote about the nature of power. Today we consider a related issue: overcoming adversity.

I abhor books that teach you to gain advantage over others by being sneaky, claiming credit for work you did not do, and keeping your colleagues uneasy or off-balance. If you encounter someone who fits that bill, refer back to Day 16, which is about escaping from cruel people. If you meet someone who tells you how much he or she loves the book *The 48 Laws of Power*—which teaches how to wield power in the ways I just mentioned—be grateful for the reveal and get away from that person.

When I was a young editor, a book made the rounds called *Power!* by publishing executive and bestselling author Michael Korda. In my brief encounters with Korda, I found him approachable and gentlemanly. (I always recall established publishing figures who were cordial to me when I was coming up—he was one.) Korda made an interesting point about worldly power and the nature of silence: he noted how corporate suites and power centers are always quiet. He said that whispering and making people lean forward when you speak is a means of asserting power in conversation. Well, you should never determine how you feel about a tactic until it gets used on you. Once as a newly minted editor I went on a visiting spree to literary agents. I stopped in at the offices of an agent at a townhouse on Manhattan's eastside. As we were speaking I became aware that she was . . . whispering. She was using one of the book's tactics. I could have gotten up and walked out. I never forgot the lesson and I never used it on another person.

There are times we all require victory in the face of adversity—when we must overcome some kind of opposition. That valid need is today's focus. But we will explore the kind of victory that is honorable, decent, and dignified. I do not want to be stepped on and I do not believe in stepping on another. If that sounds weak to you, then go read the *48 Laws*. To me, a real victory delivers me to my aim in a manner that still allows me to return home to my children as the kind of person who deserves the role of teaching them. To believe that you can function duplicitously in the world of career or commerce and honorably in the world of domesticity is a fantasy. It makes you a liar in both realms.

It is also true that life sometimes forces a confrontation upon you. It cannot always be avoided. When faced with inevitable confrontation *you will lose—unless you sincerely want to win*. Do you? Some of us are afraid to win. We fear the responsibility of being the victor, even if achieved with honor. We fear the enmity of the vanquished. We may even feel sorry for the loser. *That is not wrong*. Empathy is never negative—unless it leads to the unwarranted dissolution of self. We may feel some combination of all the things I just referenced. I have. But if you do not *want to win* you will be bulldozed. Be clear about that.

What does it mean to win? As alluded, any victory won through being a passive-aggressive creep is no victory at all. Such an approach sacrifices nobility. Concealment or phony denials of who and what you are outweigh the gain of victory. No one dies happily who goes into his or her declining years self-justifying personal underhandedness. I've seen men dying alone in hospital beds because their familial relations withered as a result of the hate they projected and practiced in the world; they thought they were compartmentalizing but it was an illusion; *you are who you are all the time*.

Hence, our goal on Day 18 is to learn how to attain victory in a decisive but honorable way.

To that end, I want you to read a widely available and accessible translation of the great Chinese ethical work *The Art of War* by Sun Tzu. I ask you to read the 1910 English translation by British sinologist Lionel Giles, which you can find online. You should also own a sturdy book edition that you can markup. Giles' translation has endured with remarkable relevance over the past century. Rather than indulge in the flourish of late-Victorian prose or the stylistic affect of King Jamesian English, Giles honored the starkness and sparseness of the original work. The economy and elegance of Giles' prose is an art form in itself.

This short work on the strategy and tactics of ancient warfare is estimated to have been written around 500 BC by the Zhou dynasty general Sun Tzu, an honorific title meaning "Master Sun." Very little is known about the author other than a historical consensus that such a figure actually existed as a commander in the dynastic emperor's army.

Like the best writing from the Taoist tradition, *The Art of War* is simple, practical, and essential. The work's insights into life and its inevitable conflicts are so organic and sound—Taoism is based on aligning with the natural order of things—that many people who have never been on a battlefield are immediately drawn into wanting to apply Sun Tzu's maxims to daily life.

I have no doubt that as you experience this slender volume you will immediately discover ideas that you want to note and use. This is because Sun Tzu's genius as a philosopher is to return us to natural principles—things that we may have once understood intuitively but lost in superfluous and speculative analysis, another of life's inevitabilities.

As you read *The Art of War* today—and it is readable in a single day—I ask that you take note of Sun Tzu's principle that the greatest warrior prevails without ever fighting. If a fighter has observed conditions, deciphered the enemy, and diligently prepared and marshaled his forces, the ideal is to overwhelm his foe without shooting a single arrow. "Supreme excellence," Sun Tzu writes, "consists in breaking the enemy's resistance without fighting." Preparation, contingency, foresight, decisiveness, and clarity often abrogate the need for direct conflict.

It if an attack does prove necessary, the master writes, it should be launched with irresistible force, like a seismic shifting of the earth. If I had to put *The Art of War* into a nutshell, I would use this one of Sun Tzu's maxims: "Let your plans be dark and impenetrable as night, and when you move, fall like a thunderbolt."

After your enemy's defeat, quickly return to normalcy. "In war then," Sun Tzu writes, "let your object be victory, not lengthy campaigns." Sun Tzu warns against protracted operations: "There is no instance of a country having benefited from prolonged warfare."

Sun Tzu teaches that the excellent commander does not seek acclaim or glory but practices subtlety, inscrutability, watchfulness, and flexibility. The effective fighter, he teaches, is like water: dwelling unnoticed at the enemy's lowest depths and striking with overwhelming force at his weakest points, the way a torrent of water rushes downhill.

Hence, the ideal preparation for attack is: 1) the practice of patience, 2) insight into your adversary's strengths and weaknesses, as well as your own, 3) study of surrounding conditions, 4) understanding and avoiding deceptions, especially those intended to lure you into hasty battle—and, finally, 5) striking with overpowering ferocity.

How do you know when to fight and when to desist? Sun Tzu's principle is: *Never fight unless victory is assured.* That is a difficult concept to abide by. Such a practice requires everything just noted, including watchfulness, forbearance, knowledge of self, knowledge of enemy, and knowledge of landscape.

I make one exception to the principle of never fighting unless victory is assured. When a matter of unshakeable honor is at stake you may be willing fight without the assurance of victory. Sometimes you must fight for principle rather than treasure. For example, I wrote the article I described in Day 6, "The Man Who Destroyed Skepticism," for free and published it with foreknowledge of the calumny it would bring. You may recall what I stated in Day 10 about not writing for free; there are exceptions for the right reasons.

In that vein, I want to reference something that Winston Churchill told a group of boarding-school students at his alma mater Harrow in 1941: "Never give in, never give in, never, never, never, never—in nothing, great or small, large or petty—never give in except to convictions of honor and good sense. Never yield to force; never yield to the apparently overwhelming might of the enemy."

Pay special attention to Sun Tzu's frequent references to adhering to the natural landscape. It is a classically Taoist approach to blend with the curvature and qualities of your surroundings—to find your place in the organic order of things. Within Vedic tradition this is sometimes called *dharma*. Napoleon Hill called it "Cosmic Habit Force." Transcendentalist philosopher Ralph

Waldo Emerson advised syncing with the patterns of nature. As the Hermetic dictum put it: "As above, so below."

Generations of readers have found Sun Tzu valuable for the manner in which he unlocks the *universality* of good strategy. What applies in warfare, if authentic, must also apply to all facets of life, including psychology. Human nature is consistent. So are the ebb and flow of events, on both macro and intimate scales.

In the end, *The Art of War* counsels victory that supports rather than disrupts the natural order of things. That is why I prefer its wisdom to the practice of winning at any cost. You cannot be right if you cannot win according to sound principles.

You must make your own assessments and applications of *The Art of War*. But I want to supply a few of its maxims that I find most meaningful. These are adapted from the Giles translation.

- Many calculations lead to victory, and few calculations to defeat: how much more no calculation at all!
- When you engage in actual fighting, if victory is long in coming, then men's weapons will grow dull and their ardor will be dampened.
- Though we have heard of stupid haste in war, cleverness has never been seen associated with long delays.

- To fight and conquer in all your battles is not supreme excellence; supreme excellence consists in breaking the enemy's resistance without fighting.

- What the ancients called a clever fighter is one who not only wins but excels in winning with ease. Hence his victories bring him neither reputation for wisdom nor credit for courage. He wins his battles *by making no mistakes*. Making no mistakes is what establishes the certainty of victory, for it means conquering an enemy that is already defeated.

- *Indirect tactics*, efficiently applied, are inexhaustible as Heaven and Earth.

- The quality of decision is like the well-timed swoop of a falcon, which enables it to strike and destroy its victim. Therefore the good fighter will be terrible in his onset and prompt in his decision.

- Whoever is first in the field and awaits the coming of the enemy will be fresh for the fight; whoever is second in the field and must hasten to battle will arrive exhausted.

- You can be sure of succeeding in your attacks if you only attack places that are *undefended*. You can ensure the safety of your defense if you only hold positions that cannot be attacked.

- *Do not repeat the tactics that have gained you one victory*, but let your methods be regulated by the infinite variety of circumstances.

- Military tactics are like unto water; for water in its natural course runs away from high places and hastens downwards.

- Just as water retains no constant shape, so in warfare are there no constant conditions.

- Let your plans be dark and impenetrable as night and when you move fall like a thunderbolt.

- Do not interfere with an army that is returning home. When you surround an army, leave an outlet free. Do not press a desperate foe too hard. [If you press a desperate person you ensure that he will fight to the death; allow a foe to disengage without losing honor.]

- Anger may in time change to gladness; vexation may be succeeded by content. But a kingdom that has once been destroyed can never come again into being; nor can the dead ever be brought back to life.

# DAY 19
## EMPATHY VERSUS SPITE

In matters of conduct, I have no taste for scholastic philosophy. I believe in practical philosophies that can—and must—be used in daily life.

The only real measure of a spiritual or ethical philosophy is its impact on conduct. What other empiricism do we possess? This is why it is insufficient in itself to call faith or religion a delusion. My response is: show me. A delusion is a dangerously depleting misconception. If you misjudge the road you crash. But if, for example, faith helps someone stop drinking or facilitates some other discernable benefit in relationship or conduct, or proves benign, then calling that outlook a delusion is merely expressing a taste. It has no objective value.

Likewise, in personal preferences or ethics, we must judge good and bad, right and wrong, banal and insightful, in ways that are discernable. Otherwise, we are arguing over labels or insignias, which may be used as identifiers but with no real meaning. In an 1898 lecture, William James observed that if one person called himself an atheist and another called himself a believer was it of any consequence? If either person learned that the world was going to end imminently, how would it affect his conduct? That, James said, is the only philosophical fulcrum we occupy.

I believe the same is true regarding what we on a personal scale call good and evil. In a summer 2020 interview, I said this to artist Josh Romero:

In terms of the human psyche there is no such thing as good and evil—there's such thing as empathy and spite. The manner in which I treat another person is the determinant of where I fall on that scale. And if I believe in some kind of personal reciprocity, which I strongly do—some people might call that karma—then it behooves me to behave responsibly toward another person. My only real moral law is not doing anything, so much as it's within my power, to interrupt or disrupt another person's search for self-potential. I simply don't understand any other operative law of ethics. It's really just about human reciprocity: am I behaving with empathy toward another or am I behaving with violence toward another? Good and evil are just badges; they're absolutely meaningless. Show them to me. It's like ego and superego—what is it? Can I put my arms around that? But I can certainly demonstrate if someone is behaving violently, either emotionally or physically, toward another person. And I have a problem with that. I can put my arms around that.

Today, Day 19, I ask you to begin applying this personal standard. Where do your hourly and daily actions fall on this scale? Too often we seek to evade questions of personal accountability by overinflating them. We seek to frame ethical questions on an epic scale of good and evil. But most of us, most of the time, do not deal with ultimates. Some of us never do. I care about what I did Tuesday. Or what I will do at 2:30 p.m. today. Because that is the proving ground of life. If your car broke down on the side of a road would you feel relieved or disheartened to see me behind the wheel of an oncoming car? Would you flag me down? Would you feel that you could count on my help (and on my ability to help)? That, and not some label or inflated framing, determines who I am.

\*    \*    \*

Do you run down other people's reputations? Use intimidation to get your way? Attack people behind their backs? Withhold responses to reasonable and timely questions? Those are the kinds of ethical issues that you and I deal with daily.

Are there larger dimensions than these to good and evil? Yes. But I framed my earlier statement in terms of the human psyche. Hence, on this day I want you to step away from evaluations other than those that are intimate. Because that is where we dwell most of the time. To avert your eyes from the intimate is generally an exercise in argumentation and hypothesizing—it avoids the self, which is the very thing that *The Miracle Month* is about.

I also structured today's exercise to address how *we often think that we are better than we really are*. The victim cries about bullies—but rarely sees the bully in him or herself. Those who frequently complain about being victimized often try to dilute their own sense of low self-worth by dragging down others with them. Often people who clamor the loudest about matters of social justice would be among the first to smack down their neighbor—*if* they held the power. I've encountered management at New Age centers that profess "progressive" politics and business ethics while not paying vendors or speakers. I knew the outspoken owner of a New Age wholesaler who fired a longtime warehouse employee because, he explained, money was lost on every order the man filled. The worker's yearly raises had made it unprofitable to employ him, he said. I don't know the solution to this problem—but I do know that it doesn't exist solely at Amazon or Walmart. The question for today is: what do I do within my own arm's reach?

When I was a child I encountered my share of bullies. I thought of myself as a victim. Yet one of the memories of which I am most ashamed is when at age 12 I used a horrible nickname for another adolescent who was deeply sensitive about her weight. I would give anything to go back and reverse that unnecessary, unthinking act of cruelty. I am so sorry for it. Being called a derogatory name, especially about something as intimate as appearance, is the very thing that adolescents bottle up; it scars them internally and can lead to a lifetime of poor self-image. I contributed to this in the life of someone who not only did nothing to me but who was actually friendly toward me at a vulnerable moment in my life. I make this confession not to be morbidly self-disclosing or self-absolving. Rather, I make it in order to *step up first* when asking you to critically ponder where you fall on the scale of empathy versus spite. *And what standard you wish to attain.* "The past controls the future, but the present controls the past."

# DAY 20
## THE POWER OF RESPECT

Years ago a magazine gave me the assignment of interviewing the coauthor of a famous book on negotiation. At first, I wasn't enthused. I expected to hear tepid bromides about communication and "getting to yes"—I questioned the applicability of the author's methods to situations of hardcore division and conflict. But I was blown away.

The writer had been working on a project aimed at reducing violence in prisons. He observed that the vast majority of fights between inmates arose from the perception of disrespect. "Respect," he said, "is the cheapest thing you can possibly extend to another person. It costs nothing. But the results can change everything."

I want you to think very carefully about that today. Events in extreme environments reflect a graduated scale of events in more normative ones. Scan your life and interactions—including on social media, emails, and texts—for areas where you withhold respect. This can occur in seemingly benign ways, such as by not thanking someone over email or text. Or it can come in the form of needless sarcasm or eyerolls, especially in social media posts. Or simply not acknowledging another person as you would like to be acknowledged. Recall William James's letter about appreciation in Day 17.

The decision to respect people will improve, alter, and, depending on the circumstances, potentially save your life. Your task today, Day 20, is to demonstrate respect as a deliberate choice and in all situations.

As of this writing, I live on the Lower East Side of Manhattan. Some people think I live on a sketchy block. A fair number of people are usually out on the streets, some of whom do not have regular homes. Drugs are a common presence. At night I walk with purpose and keep my eyes sharp. In addition, I show respect toward people on the streets. The vast majority of the time most people are simply looking to be treated decently. If someone is sleeping or passed out in my building's doorway I ask him to move—but he will be addressed as "my man" or "brother" and spoken to as a person. Without excessive deference—which indicates fear not respect—and with dignity. Just as I would wish to be spoken to. I teach this to my sons.

Once in a while I experience crises of respect on the street. Usually they arise from stress. One night in my neighborhood I was in a rush and I walked with my bike in between two cars with my helmet strapped at my side. My helmet bumped one of the cars. A few moments later the driver yelled for me to watch my you-know-what helmet. I paused for a moment realizing what had happened and said, "Sorry." His car crawled a bit of a way up the block and he yelled back at me a derogatory name. I paused again. I weighed responding or confronting him. I kept silent. I knew that if I risked confrontation it could easily escalate. Once that happens you never know what will occur and I possess too much in life to throw it away over nonsense. That is what I mean in the section on anger about pitting one emotion against another. I walked away. Understanding respect also means knowing what it's worth to you and having perspective on the greater good.

Consider a different kind of encounter. None of us like speaking to customer service reps. But are you respectful to them? They have tough jobs. They are trained to give a limited retinue of responses. Truth be told, I hate being on such calls. But I do all that I can to speak to the person as if he or she were seated in the same room with me. These reps do not set policy. And they sit through a lot of frustration and complaints. It is a draining and not especially well-paying job. The person who shows them respect stands out. A display of respect and kindness makes their hour or workday. And everyone, from police officers to the customer service rep, has greater latitude in their jobs than might be imagined. A personal bond gets you places that surliness never will. Indeed surliness, in any situation, may get you someplace you desperately do not want to go. Apropos of the example I gave earlier, recall the aphorism from *The Art of War*: "Anger may in time change to gladness; vexation may be succeeded by content. But a kingdom that has once been destroyed can never come again into being; nor can the dead ever be brought back to life."

I was once driving on the Taconic State Parkway in New York's Hudson Valley and accelerated to pass another driver who was swerving. I wanted to get away from him. Bam—a state trooper pulled me over for speeding. We had a respectful exchange and she advised me to take the ticket to court, explaining that the judge would probably not give me points on my license. Although the trip to court was distant from home and inconvenient, I complied because points would spike my insurance rates. The ticket itself was about $200, no small matter either. In the crowded waiting area people sat shoulder-to-shoulder waiting first to see a prosecutor and then to see a judge. In a room of about 300 people there were workers, soldiers, parents with kids, people from every walk of life—all of them with one aim: leniency.

When my turn came to speak with the prosecutor, I spoke with her respectfully and with relatability— neither cloying nor officious, just one to one, person to person. She had a hard job and I knew it. When I explained what occurred, she asked: "Do you promise to drive for the rest of your life like a little old lady?" I heartily agreed. "Okay," she said, "I'm letting you off." No fine, no points, no nothing. I walked. I was obviously grateful but also felt saddened. There is without question a degree of injustice in this. The room was packed with people who were no more or less deserving than I—and many for whom the points or fine were graver matters. I am not blind to the social dimensions. But at the same time the ability to see that prosecutor not as a foe but as someone with a serious job and her own needs—and to show her attendant respect—helped settle the matter in a way that I hadn't even hoped for.

You simply do not know the payoff or price of respect and its opposite, and how or when it will arrive. Approach the matter carefully.

When we disrespect another person it is sometimes out of obliviousness—probably the most common cause—and sometimes because we believe we are entitled to something that the person is not giving us. Disrespect may occur in the form of abrupt or rude replies; its withholding can be as perilous as its offering is efficacious.

Let me offer another street story. Years ago in New York City I was having dinner with friends in an outdoor seating area at an Indian restaurant in the East Village. Street life in the East Village was not what you'd call relaxing at the time and I was skeptical when a friend said that he wanted to sit outside but nonetheless complied. Shortly after sitting down, we were approached for money a man "selling" freebie newspapers that used to be dispensed in New York at corner kiosks. Urban dwellers face this kind of thing frequently and it is the individual's decision to give or not give, with valid reasons on either side. This was a time not to. I began to politely decline. My friend, however, spoke over me and said, "NO, NO, *we're not interested.*" Immediately the man's face darkened and body tensed. He stuck his face into mine—I wasn't the one who had spoken but I was seated on the street-side of our table. He threatened to break my jaw. I don't scare easily on the street but, again, I know when to avoid foolish confrontations. I don't recall exactly what I said but I deescalated the situation telling him that I understood but we had nothing for him. He walked off.

That episode, its potential for violence, and its cooldown, hinged entirely *on tone.*

Not all of us hear our tone. People sometimes poke fun at the idea of paying excessive attention to tone. Jerry Seinfeld does a hilarious standup bit about how as a parent your tone is constantly monitored. But tone conveys more than words. A simple, plain, and respectful decline would have allowed the man in my story to walk away. But when you make someone feel reduced, that person, either in the moment or later, feels that something must been set right, and that can occur through violence, confrontation, or passive-aggression.

Or, the individual may have no direct opportunity for protest or recompense—but what have you gained? You perpetuate your own atonality and ensure that the injured party will displace his hurt onto another.

If you do not hear yourself when you talk you must bring attention to your tone. It is the vital conveyance of respect or disrespect. If you want lessons in respect, watch any movie starring Jimmy Stewart. The affable actor possessed the uncanny ability to speak to other characters and his audience with familial ingenuousness and congeniality. He never seemed syrupy, manipulative, or cloying. He made others feel that they could let down their guard. Study his cadences if you need to. The larger point is to listen, perhaps for the first time, to how you address others, and to measure this subtle but vital element of life.

Up to this point, I have focused mostly on personal and spoken encounters. With most office work having migrated online as of this writing, and with social media the chief vehicle for interpersonal activity and relationships, written communication desperately requires a new set of rules. An entire book could be written on this topic alone. I will limit myself to a few key observations, which I ask you to put into action today.

Almost every email you write comes across more abruptly than intended. This is due to the issues of tone that I noted earlier. Tone, in its original meaning, is audible. It conveys greater meaning than words. Conventional terms like *please, thank you,* or *you're welcome* can be polite or sarcastic based on cadence. Since email is atonal the recipient projects his or her own perceptions onto what you've written. Hence, unless you are trying to be obnoxious (which runs counter to today's lesson) it benefits you in emails, texts, or posts to ensure that you use proper salutations and take extra steps toward politeness even in seemingly minor messages. Use someone's name, greet them appropriately, and sign off with regards.

If you have any doubts about the power of cordiality in human relations read Dale Carnegie's 1936 book *How to Win Friends and Influence People*. Carnegie's insights into human nature, including its vanity and emotional fragility, translate not only perfectly but also urgently to our digital era. Even though digital commerce was generations away from his time, Carnegie, a shrewd student of human nature, effectively foresaw the challenges of an era dominated by written, real-time communication. Use his insights in every pixelated note or post you make.

Everything I write here applies more generally on social media. I am not a perfect actor on social media. Emotions sometimes take the reins. But I must tell you: if you make a habit or even occasional practice of demeaning or running down people on social media it will return to haunt you. Random rudeness gets taken out of your skin in ways that you'll never anticipate. People you may not suspect are reading your social media feeds. You may think anonymity shields you. Think again. I believe there is an even greater cost in self-respect and self-perception when you rundown people from behind the wall of digital anonymity. You will never respect yourself if you say things on social media that you would not say to someone's face. It serves only to deepen the divide between who you may wish to be and who you are.

"Let thine eye by single"—apply that principle to the digital age. Be the same individual in written and face-to-face communication and you will stand taller. And let that person show not deference but respect. Respecting another will come to your rescue in ways that you may not perceive.

# DAY 21
## ONE THING DONE RIGHT

On September 26, 2020, I posted the following on Twitter and Instagram:

I know a lot of people are suffering during this lockdown. If you email me via my website I will send you a free PDF of my short book, *Depression and Metaphysics*. This is not some lame attempt to harvest email addresses. I don't keep emails or send promo announcements.

I heard from a lot of great people and got a lot of grateful comments. But I would estimate that upwards of five percent of respondents proved unwilling or incapable of following even the minor ask in the post that you write me via my website. They requested the book through DM, replied to the post, asked for my email, or introduced some other wrinkle. Someone took the liberty of posting my email on Instagram as a matter of convenience. I ignored these responses because if you cannot meet even the minor bar set for receiving something free, you will take none of the more significant steps in the book.

Today's exercise actually comes in the form of an aphorism. It was shared with me by a former boss, and I always found it valuable: *The way you do one thing is the way you do everything.* It has never failed me. If you take it seriously, it will provide you with insight, guidance, and self-correction.

Do you know what an em-dash is? It is a copyediting term for a long dash used to separate clauses in a sentence or to offset the source of a quote. It looks like this: —. It is not a broken dash (--) or a smaller dash that goes between words, varyingly called a hyphen or en-dash. In more than twenty years in publishing I could always tell who was going to excel and who was going to prove mediocre. The proving ground was a writer, editor, or designer's willingness to grasp this small distinction. I have explained it to people who gazed back at me with an expression of blankness. Yet such things are not obsessive nits. They are the finishing touches that render your work complete and signal that you care about the reader's experience. This small step—no smaller in its realm than properly tightening a screw on an aircraft assembly line—provided a near-infallible litmus test.

One of the principles that I love with Taoism and Zen is what might be called *alignment*. The time spent crafting, cleaning, or caring for a household item, devising the layout of a room, or even a setting a table for a meal is intended to bring one's surroundings into harmony with the natural order of things. The individual can feel and experience this in his or her own encounter with an item, object, or condition—alignment produces a feeling of ease, peace, relaxation, and settlement. The perfection of the one thing is the perfection of the whole.

Even you feel unmoved to pass through life with the meticulousness of a Zen master it remains possible and, I believe, necessary to live from the same general principle. This principle may not always prevail—life sometimes distracts you from a certain task like housekeeping—but the general idea is that if you take on a effort, large or small, you ought to treat it like something that expresses who you fully are, which is actually the truth.

In his biography of Steve Jobs, Walter Isaacson tells the story of Jobs handling an iPod prototype. When Jobs plugged headphones into the AUX port he immediately rejected the model. Jobs insisted that the user should feel a secure, satisfying "click" when snapping a jack into a port. That was missing. He sent the model back to the engineers. People could roll their eyes, and I'm sure a few did, but Jobs was drawing upon factors of natural instinct, engineering excellence, customer satisfaction—and also his own study of Zen, aesthetics, architecture, and utility. This is the kind of excellence I am asking you to practice today.

There is an ethical dimension to this question, as well. A person who lies once is apt to lie generally. It is a tough truth. I learned from observation that if you witness someone lying to another person—in matters large or small—you can count on the fact that he is also lying to you or eventually will.

Early in my publishing career a colleague and I recommended a writer to the organizers of a spiritual conference who were seeking a keynote speaker. The conference planners took our recommendation and paid the speaker several thousand dollars. But following the event one of them later called us to say that they were unhappy with the speaker's performance. The writer was specifically asked not to read from one of his books on stage—he read anyway. I learned from him that he also harbored his own misgivings about the event and it clearly wasn't a good pairing. As we spoke with the conference organizer over speakerphone, however, my colleague said something that was untrue. He told the organizer that the same writer had recently spoken at another conference—that much was true—and that the hosts were very happy and "want him back." I knew that to be false. The other engagement was, in fact, modestly attended. No one complained but no future invites were extended. My colleague was saying that tactically to diminish the organizer's complaints. The same colleague also used that tactic on me. I didn't always realize it at the time. Other times I avoided acknowledging it to myself to preserve comity. But looking back I knew that what I witnessed that day was a blueprint. *The way you do one thing is the way you do everything.*

I do not mean to describe this truth only as a negative. There are hidden tendrils in life that work to your advantage. If you accept my point then it stands to reason that fixing one thing in life—even a small matter—will make itself felt in myriad and larger ways. I grew up in a household that was dominated by a somewhat finicky, selfish standard of behavior. Favors and acts of consideration were rare. I attempt not to repeat this cycle with my own children. The day that I am writing these words one of my kids asked me to pick him up pizza while I was on a bike ride. It's unwieldy carrying a pizza box on a bike but rather than prevaricate I immediately agreed. It was, of course, a small act. But my hope is that that kind of small act, for him, for me, for our domicile, sets the template for greater and steadier acts of consideration.

Large changes stem from small changes. And there is a reason for that: life is a continuum, always and in everything.

Take this day to do small things in the right way. Watch carefully for how a seemingly small act fans outward. The effect may appear suddenly or over time. But it will appear. And cumulatively. Make today's small fix the basis of a larger life.

# DAY 22
## REJECT COMFORT MEDIA

**W**e derive a visceral thrill and probably a dopamine rush from reading things that affirm what we already believe. This is especially true of emotional subjects like religion and politics. "Opinion porn," if I may, delivers the same kind of repetitive thrill as binge eating. It provides the head-nodding jolt of seeing your imagined adversaries taken down and your team score another touchdown.

Beware of this pattern. The repeat-intake of opinioneering stifles original thought even as you believe you are receiving more and more insight. (Hint: insight doesn't arrive in quantity.) In actuality, bingeing on opinion-affirming media is an emotional and physical fix more than an intellectual one, even though the tools are words, facts, and arguments. It is ersatz learning, no more nutritious to your intellect than consuming a bag of chips is to your body—and probably with equivalent health costs over time.

The thrill of familiar victory, the smackdown of the other side drives millions of clicks to political blogs and online journals. Yes, some facts and news bits get dispensed along the way; but the real draw is the *feeling* you get when once again pulling the polemical slots handle and re-upping the excitement that accompanies *being right*.

Today's goal is to pull the plug on habitually reading opinion-adjacent news or political media. Reject "comfort media." That doesn't mean a news or opinion blackout. Nor does it mean supplementing your intake with material you disagree with, which itself may have no special value. Rather, it means choosing quality over quantity in your current-events reading.

I keep up with politics and current events. I check several news sites, chiefly *The New York Times*, often a few times a day. I might skim a few other places. In full disclosure, I read the daily horoscope in the *New York Post*. (I like astrologer Sally Brompton, what can I tell you?) If friends or my kids send me news links, I often read them. But I make little time for commentary or opinion blogs. I virtually never watch video links people send me. I have zero time for most smackdown clips or anything close. Cumulatively it's just too great a time suck.

*How do you know when you're imbibing comfort media?* Repetition. It's when the argument is one you've read before and are reading again to restore a sense of validation.

For example, many social critics today, from best-selling writers to bloggers, write "take down" pieces about *The Secret* (now fourteen years old!) and New Age culture with almost habitual regularity. It's easy. You can always poke holes in ethereal claims and shout "confirmation bias" (without asking whether you've applied the principle to yourself). And it's old. Iconic social and literary critic H.L. Mencken (1880–1956) took mind metaphysics for numerous trips to the woodshed more than a century ago. For example, on December 3, 1910, the columnist wrote a piece called "Mental Vibrations" in the *Baltimore Evening Sun*:

> The New Thought, that fantastic magic, goes marching on . . . There is, in brief, little if any truth in the belief that good wishes may be transformed into objective phenomena, that mind influences matter— and little, even, in the belief that mind influences mind. Actors and opera singers often do their worst work in the presence of absurdly friendly crowds,

and their best in the presence of crowds which sit silent and unmoved.

The critic added: "As a matter of fact, the very best efforts of many men, perhaps of the majority of those men whose efforts are worth anything at all, are inspired by opposition as much as by huzzahs." As a "believing historian" of alternative spirituality, I agree with him on that count; but my definition of New Thought is not really positive thinking in the see-no-evil sense as it is determined thinking. As I've widely explored, I believe that thoughts possess causative properties and that life operates under both physical and extra-physical principles. We live under many laws and forces. What's more, in matters of personal philosophy I look twice at rejected stones. As carpenters say: measure twice, cut once.

Of course, none of this means I'm right and the Baltimore Bard is wrong. It means that if conceptually you've read it before, ask: is it worth it? Do we need one more article (or book) to decry what Mencken laid his formidable glove on more than a century ago? Generally speaking, unless a social or political critique is notably fresh or urgent, it's *comfort media*.

Use this as a guideline: if you are spending more than two hours a day reading or viewing news-related content, you are likely wasting valuable time. It probably isn't necessary to spend more than a couple of hours a day, give or take, to stay informed. (Unless there's a special event, like a presidential debate.) More than that, I venture, is task-avoidance and frivolity rather than productivity and learning.

Consider the possibilities of freeing up the time you spend on comfort-zone media—it could easily be one, two, or even three hours a day. What would you do with that time? You could exercise, meditate, cook, work, spend time with a loved one, or read something of lasting quality.

*Participate in the culture and not the commentary.*

# DAY 23
## PRACTICE SEX TRANSMUTATION

This one of the more occultic exercises in this book. It requires no leap of faith into mystical realms but only a simple, experimental effort practiced privately and on your own terms.

This method is called "sex transmutation."

In short, sex transmutation means *selectively directing your feelings of sexual arousal away from physical satisfaction and toward the completion of a cherished task*, such as a work of art, the solution to a problem, the repair or design of a device, an act of calculus, and so on. This practice places heightened acumen, enthusiasm, and energy at the back of your efforts. Or so goes the theory. I think you will find it true.

To be clear: the act of sex transmutation is performed at moments of your choosing and does not require abstinence; it is a periodic, elective experiment.

I first discovered this exercise in the work of success writer Napoleon Hill (1883–1970), author of *Think and Grow Rich*. Sex transmutation is one of Hill's most subtle, powerful, and intriguing techniques. In 1948, Hill wrote in *Think Your Way to Wealth*:

> The emotion of sex is nature's own source of inspiration through which she gives both men and women the impelling desire to create, build, lead, and direct. Every great artist, every great musician, and every great dramatist gives expression to the emotion of sex transmuted into human endeavor.

Hill argued that the urge toward sexuality is *the creative impulse of life expressing itself through the individual*. In that vein, Hill taught that sexuality goes beyond intimacy and reproduction; rather, it is the expansive principle of life at the back of every effort of human creativity. There is antecedent for his observation in many different spiritual traditions: Taoism, Kabbalah, Vedic teachings, and modern-day chaos and ceremonial magick. Indeed, sex transmutation is the aspect of Hill's philosophy that most fully comports to other wisdom traditions and it is the most esoteric.

Consider this: we are driven to function as creative, generative beings in myriad ways—commercially, artistically, relationally, and in communication, travel, culture, and civics. Whenever you strive to actualize your visions in the world you are operating from a universal, generative impulse toward expansion. Without it we would stagnate.

Once you cultivate this awareness, Hill taught, you can actually transmute the generative—or as he saw it procreative or sexual—impulse into the strengthening and refinement of skills and focus required for a given task. Let me repeat his method: When you experience the sexual impulse you redirect your thoughts and energies along the lines of a cherished project or piece of work. Through the mental act of redirecting yourself from physical satisfaction to creative expression you harness and place the sexual urge at the back of whatever you wish to achieve. This, Hill taught, adds intellectual power, vigor, and insight to your efforts.

At the core of his exercise is the gambit that the sexual urge, which is universally felt but narrowly defined, can be harnessed in ways that surpass physical releases. This practice does not *replace* physical satisfaction but provides an alternative outlet selected at times of your choosing and manner. Once you discover that *you as an individual are capable of redirecting sexual desire towards an expression other than the physical* you may then resume or return to the physical whenever you wish.

We often hear term "alchemy" used to describe the transformation or refinement of physical or psychological material. Sex transmutation is, in effect, an act of mental alchemy. This transmutation or rechanneling of one impulse—sexuality—to another use—creativity— does, in my experience, add intellect, enthusiasm, focus, and intuitive insight to whatever you are working on. Sex transmutation consciously places the force of creation itself at the back of your personal efforts. You can determine the applicability of that statement through experience.

I must restate that sex transmutation in Hill's rendering does not require you to sublimate or repress the sexual urge. Indeed, Hill emphasizes that nothing is greater tonic for one's mood, spirit, and physical relaxation and wellness than healthfully expressed physical sexuality. He is noting that there exist other channels through which sexuality is also expressed. Physical expression is vital; but there are creative, artistic, athletic, and intellectual channels through which the impulse can likewise be directed. In fact, we are doing this all the time, albeit unknowingly. When you feel "seduced" by a salesperson that is part of what is occurring.

I want to provide a brief historical note before returning to the practical aspect of Day 23. I have written both critically and supportively of Hill's work. Over the years, critics have complained that Hill's notion of success is too single-minded or outwardly focused. (I challenge that, as Hill's programmatic ethics run deeper than detected.) Others point to questionable aspects of his biography. (Such as whether he really met and interviewed industrialist Andrew Carnegie, who never mentions Hill in his memoirs. I'm agnostic on this point.) And still others note Hill's tendency to favor the powerful while running down policies of social equity. (I join in that criticism.) But these critiques, while valid to varying degrees, are blunted by the remarkable effectiveness of Hill's program. I state that from private experience and collaboration with others.

Those who are interested in esoteric spirituality may wonder at the connection between Hill's sex transmutation and the contemporary practice of what is called sex magick. In its most basic form, sex magick involves setting an intention at the point of climax, although there are other iterations, which include forestalling climax or abstinence. In many cases, ceremony or ritual is used. But a lot of what we call ceremonial magick, chaos magick, or other forms of spell work could be considered New Thought—or mind causation—practiced along ritualized lines. Indeed, the basic premise behind most modern magick is that the will can be externalized and desires can be out-pictured through rite, focus, symbol, sexuality, and ceremony. Sex transmutation comports with both magick and New Thought.

As noted, the principle of sex transmutation has appeared in esoteric tradition for ages; it got popularized in the late-nineteenth and early-twentieth centuries by figures including occultist Paschal Beverly Randolph and artist and magician Aleister Crowley. Their efforts laid the tracks for a good deal of ceremonial magick today. I have no reason to believe that Hill was directly aware of their work or that of related figures and groupings, such as the Hermetic Order of the Golden Dawn. Certainly he left no such references. But Hill did bring an esoteric interpretation of his own to sex transmutation.

Hill posited that sex energy is the force behind genius itself. For the plural term geniuses, Hill used the arcane plural *genii*. Genii dates to Roman-Latin usage. It not only means intellectual prowess but also suggests the Ancient Roman meaning that genius itself is a gift bestowed by numinous forces or daemons. The same term appears as *jinn* or genie in Arab folklore and culture, again referencing a spirit capable of either possessing the individual or bestowing supernatural power. This suggests the connection Hill saw between greater forces of life and the individual's capacity for accomplishment.

I must add that it is unnecessary to accept any of these premises in order to perform today's exercise. But I do like to provide some of the thought history and philosophical rationale behind spiritual practices. Our interest is to *use* the practice—today. And if you find sufficient reason, which I believe you will, you can carry it with you from this point forward.

# DAY 24
## PRESENT RIGHT

am a huge fan of Brian Wilson, the songwriter, arranger, and producer who cofounded The Beach Boys. Wilson expanded our conception of what pop music could be. Although The Beach Boys are famous for infectious, feel-good hits about surfing and hot rods, Wilson's orchestrations and production values combined classical motifs with pop riffs and produced some of the most uncategorizable music of our time, including the 1966 experimental masterpiece *Pet Sounds*. The album represented a breakthrough expansion of the pop sound and production. Wilson also brought a new degree of lyrical introspection to the genre with songs like, "I Just Wasn't Made for These Times" and "That's

Not Me." *Pet Sounds* served as a precursor to *Sgt. Pep-per's Lonely Hearts Club Band* and much else. I consider Brian Wilson the Orson Welles of rock.

The songwriter's work ethic was as legendary as his output was original. "Brian was between a hipster and one of your famous British generals that was tough," recalled bandmate Bruce Johnston in a documentary about the making of *Pet Sounds*. "He was tough. He demanded everything from everybody."

Yet when Wilson and bandmate Mike Love presented the finished recording to Capitol Records the music giant's executives were unenthusiastic. They wanted the earlier songs about summer nights and fun. Although The Beatles had already proven that an expanded pop sound could sell, the label wanted The Beach Boys to remain in their lane. Keep making feel-good hits.

Capitol agreed to release the record but did so unenthusiastically. The label arranged a maudlin, almost silly-looking cover shoot of Brian and his bandmates feeding barnyard animals at the San Diego Zoo. The syrupy cover photo belies everything that appears on the grooves within. It took twenty years for *Pet Sounds* to go platinum and finally receive the critical and fan recognition it deserved.

I have often wondered what would have occurred if Brian—who struggled with severe anxiety and depression—had pushed back against the record company's lame packaging. Image says so much. With a more conceptual cover, like the Beatles' contemporaneous *Rubber Soul*, fans and the music business in general might have been quicker to embrace *Pet Sounds*.

In his book *Wouldn't It Be Nice*, a history of *Pet Sounds*, writer Charles L. Granata spoke with Mike Love about Paul McCartney's response to the cover. McCartney has repeatedly singled out the album for praise, cited its influence on the Beatles, and offered that "I've just bought my kids each a copy of it for their education in life—I figure no one is educated musically 'til they've heard that album." But here is what he told Love about the packaging:

> Paul McCartney and I spoke about the album in the spring of 1968 when we were in India together. [The two were practitioners of Transcendental Meditation and were visiting the Maharishi's ashram in Rishikesh.] In one conversation, he mentioned that we ought to take more care with our album covers. Paul was the mastermind behind the *Sgt. Pepper* album cover, which was detailed and brilliant. Ours . . . was a photo taken at the San Diego Zoo. That indicated how comprehensively Paul thought of everything. We didn't think about the packaging—we were never marketed thoughtfully, like the Beatles. That

was partly our own fault, for not thinking as comprehensively as they did.

Are you thinking comprehensively about how you are presenting yourself, your persona, and your ideas and work in the world?

Of course, image alone is insufficient. Every poet, actor, singer, and artist who you admire is known for one primary reason (or ought to be): quality of output. Admittedly, we live in an era of Internet stardom where sometimes appearance alone makes a celebrity. But take away the platform—remember Vine?—and the person with one million followers can vanish as suddenly as if he or she never existed.

The lesson of Day 24 is: *let your work speak; let your image punctuate.* Both are necessary. Both must be cultivated. The direction of one should contain the other. Think comprehensively. Present right.

One of the most potent examples I know of work and image coinciding appears in the career of *The Twilight Zone* creator, writer, and host Rod Serling (1924–1975). Someone once observed of Serling that he was one of the few writers who "looked like his material." He had an urbane, mysterious quality and a beautiful, deep, sonorous voice. Serling was enigmatic on camera—the perfect guide to draw us in with the famous opener,

"There is a fifth dimension beyond that which is known to man . . ." Not every one of us have screen presence or need to. But I do think that cultivating a total image—one based on quality of work and a self-determined, synchronous outer appearance—helps you get noticed. And noticed for the right things.

Let me return for a moment to The Beach Boys. Years after *Pet Sounds*, when the band had already left its old label, Capitol decided to release a Beach Boys Greatest Hits Vol. 3. It was exactly the kind of conventional treatment that Wilson chaffed against. And it sounded lame: how can a "greatest hit" appear in a third-tier volume? This time lead singer Love spoke up and approached Capitol with a different idea. Call the record *Endless Summer*, he said. The new title evoked the ethos the band was after: dreamy, hopeful, and also elusive. It summoned the past without being tied to it. Capitol agreed and *Endless Summer*, which otherwise might have been headed for the bargain bin as Greatest Hits Vol. 3, went triple-platinum and became one of the top-selling albums of 1974. It ignited a wave of new interest in the band. My big sister owned the double-album and I may not have otherwise discovered The Beach Boys.

Perhaps I've brushed past a deeper truth, noted not by The Beach Boys but by literary lion H.L. Mencken in 1912: "Style, after all, is inseparable from content, however the stylists may seek to make it appear not so." When your work is of quality your style will often (if sometimes belatedly) follow. Cultivate this process. Whatever you do that is distinctive, brilliant, and capable should be married to the proper image. This is done not to curry favor but to contextualize content. *Pet Sounds* was a revolutionary work hampered by poor packaging. Yet a potentially throwaway record, *Endless Summer*, was lifted to mass sales and notice by its evocative title. Hip hop artists often prove masterful at the process I am describing. Study them.

However much we may overlook the fact or push it away, *image and packaging matter*. Bring this focus to your work from this point forward.

Let me add a personal note. Once I was shopping for a vintage leather jacket in connection with a television shoot. I opted for one that fit me too tightly to zip close. When I got home I was unsure I had made the right choice—who wears a jacket that cannot close?

Someone told me, "The Ramones couldn't close their jackets either. Just look at their album covers." Suddenly I realized what attracted me to it, albeit unconsciously. The jacket looked street without being bulky, sleek without seeming stylized. It captured the punk elegiac image I wanted to bring to my discussion of the occult and also represented my roots. You can see the jacket on the cover of this book and *The Miracle Habits*. I married image and content—and did so authentically.

A final dimension of this principle is in *rejecting facsimiles*.

Think for a moment of a cultural or historical figure whom you admire. The names that immediately come to mind for me are political leader Jawaharlal Nehru (1889–1964), artist Frida Kahlo (1907–1954), and architect Frank Lloyd Wright (1867–1959). If you consider or search each figure's appearance and image you will quickly realize that it was *entirely original*. They didn't copy; they were copied. They were the culture and not the commentary. The collarless "Nehru suit" that I mentioned in Day 1 is named for the East-meets-West couture of the Indian leader. Secondary? Not to him. Part of Nehru's governing appeal in India was his ability to blend into his clothing aspects from each faith—Hindu, Buddhist, Muslim—and to dress in ways that spoke to both traditionalists and young people who wanted closer ties to the West. Style is not incidental.

We dwell not only in a thought world but a consumer one in which it is all-too-easy to attempt to purchase a self-image off the shelf. But that rarely satisfies. And it is often deleteriously expensive, creating a cycle of repeat and fruitless purchases. This is among the reasons that

I advise assembling a personal uniform on Day 1. To the greatest extent possible, you must create yourself and your surroundings from what you make, adjust, hack, retrofit, reuse, design, and mix-and-match. This commitment has a greater impact on your persona than may first appear.

As noted in the introduction, I see no natural division between so-called inner and outer, higher and lower, material and spiritual, personality and essence— life is a whole. The boundaries that we draw are, I believe, artifice, which get reinforced through repetition and translation of translation of spiritual ideas that we consider template but that must, if they are to play an authentic function in our lives, be reinvestigated by every searching individual. Virtually every spiritual principle of self-development, whatever its vintage, originated in an atmosphere of specific cultural and human needs, and requires reverification.

Moreover, I venture that the feelings of confidence and self-possession you experience when you are "in your element," whether in terms of people, surroundings, or adornment, should not be undervalued or ignored. They are clues to the wholeness of life and the manner in which everything is innately connected. Alter one element and you alter them all, however subtly.

\*          \*          \*

There is a bar I love in my home borough of Queens, New York. It is a hangout for artists, promoters, actors, filmmakers, and musicians; its regulars all possess a gloriously distinctive and seemingly effortless look. Nothing is really effortless, of course. The quality that the bargoers bring to their personal appearance is *originality of form*, married to work and output. Tattoos, clothing, painted jackets, decals, pins, boots—all are items that the wearers labored to find, reclaim from original sources (remember my jacket?), or get designed for them, and then combine in ways that have never quite been done before. Everyone is wholly him or herself.

I want you today to see yourself as a canvas that only you design. It may take time. There is no map. There are no specific rules other than: *reject facsimiles*. Do you want a .45 handgun tie clip? Get the real kind, the one you saw your uncle wearing that time, which maybe he had gotten from his local gun club. This kind of thing, while seemingly small, weens you away from packaged aesthetics, and, in time, packaged opinions and ideas. It makes you search rather than buy, strive rather than absorb, and preserve rather than consume. The bar I mentioned? The day before writing these words I saw someone there wearing a jacket with the words painted on the back: "Build Something Out of Nothing." Take that as today's motto.

# DAY 25
## LEAVE THE AIRPORT

When you are faced with a crisis—and life can sometimes feel like a series of crises—nothing vanishes faster than your own sense of power and agency. Yet you possesses greater sway over events and other people than you believe—if that sway is used constructively.

I am writing these words from the Yucatan in Mexico, where I ventured to celebrate the birthday of my partner.* The arrival was fraught with difficulties: Our initial flight was canceled due to a hurricane. When we flew the following day we were digesting the emotional

---

* I tested positive for antibodies before the trip and traveled masked and following all safety protocols.

fallout of a business arrangement that had gone awry. We arrived to find a crowded and somewhat unsettling scene at the airport, which was filled with delayed and rerouted travelers. We had a rental car reserved but were unable to locate the desk or a shuttle stop. Confusion abounded as the region was still recovering from the storm, which was milder than expected but nonetheless serious. We began hearing rumors that our slightly off-brand rental agency was closed. We had paid in advance and, wary of losing the fee or succumbing to hearsay, we thought about just taking a cab to its lot in order to try our luck and cut our loss. But information was sketchy and phone service was spotty. Standing outside the airport, we were being closed in on by taxi drivers, tour guides, rental agents, and various pitchmen trying to get us to follow them. If you've ever been in that situation you know it can feel disorienting. Emotions were already running high and were about to boil over.

I suddenly spotted a van for a major car rental company that just pulled up to the curb. We had no reservation with them. I said to my partner: "Let's just get in." I realized that above all else we needed to get out of that airport and away from the pushiness and prying of hustlers who knew we were in trouble. (Mind you, I have no brief against them—they have needs and jobs, too.) If the major rental company couldn't provide a car, its lot would surely be situated in a hub with other rental agencies and we would somehow get a car and get on our way. As for the AWOL car company we had paid in advance, we could take that up with our credit card company later. The key thing was to stabilize the situation. We *had* to get out of that airport.

Once we arrived at the name-brand car agency everything clicked into place. Had we lingered where things were chaotic we would've gotten taken advantage of. The story would've ended very differently.

In the scheme of things, this is a very small episode. But small episodes teach you about dealing with larger ones. Lesson one: It is vital to act. To use your power. Sometimes acting may mean purposefully waiting, being patient, and gathering information. A great deal of activity occurs in silence or in seeming repose. That is how a lizard hunts. The Tao Te Ching says: "Timing is everything." Never neglect that. Whatever your course, nothing is worse than avoidance, indecision, or freezing. In my publishing days I used to tell writers that if they were experiencing difficulty in meeting a deadline come to me and we'll work it out together. The worst thing you can do is prevaricate.

Today, Day 25, you must "leave the airport." Identify some difficulty you are experiencing in life, large or small. Then remind yourself—*because it is true*—that you possess greater power and agency than you realize.

Respect and abide by that power. Make a decision. Act. *Do something.*

That doing is not narrowly proscribed. It may involve diplomacy, apology, redoing, refusal, labor, or seeking information. In a certain sense, it is to your advantage if the problem you address is relatively small because part of today's exercise is to realize once more that *what you do on a micro scale can be repeated on a macro scale.* Life is symmetrical. Again, the Hermetic dictum: "As above, so below."

Naturally a person may face physical barriers or overwhelming crises that will not yield, at least not apparently or fully, to personal action. But we so rarely stand fully tall. We slide into panic, despair, passivity, or avoidance. Today's point is to *try.* I admire this observation from journalist Norman Cousins in his *Anatomy of an Illness*, which I believe can be broadly interpreted: "Not every illness can be overcome. But many people allow illness to disfigure their lives more than it should. They cave in needlessly. They ignore and weaken whatever powers they have for standing erect."

Get accustomed to running into the wind rather than avoiding it.

Act—and you will discover greater dimensions than you suspect.

# DAY 26
## DO YOU ENJOY SUFFERING?

The greatest barrier to your happiness is often the secret pleasure that you derive from suffering.

Does that sound absurd or affected? It is not. Human beings are generally selfish. When you repeat something over and over there is usually a principle of self-gain at work even in areas that appear fraught with pain.

I had a close family member who constantly—even in the midst of good times and, it seemed, especially in the midst of them—would emotionally pull grenade pins. She would do things that could only and inevitably cause arguments and hurt feelings. I witnessed this behavior during or immediately following family gatherings that were otherwise marked by comity and relative peace. It was a pattern. With regularity, either during a social event or the next day, she would blow things up with an inappropriate remark or gratuitous demand. I often tried to speak with her about this to elucidate and ameliorate the pattern. But to no avail. At such times, she would profess no understanding of what I was describing. After years of fruitless communication, it finally occurred to me: this person was enjoying what was going on. She found conflict thrilling and empowering.

Spiritual teacher Vernon Howard called this "a false feeling of life." It is related to the sensation one gets when viewing violence, firing a gun, or tweeting out a bilious comment. It can be addictive. And devastatingly fractious when applied to relationships.

The person I described was a family intimate. But shame on me if I am not equally probing of myself. Because today, Day 26, I am asking you to do the same. This may be the most important day of our month together.

I am writing these words from Tulum, Mexico. Last night I had the privilege of participating in a sweat-lodge ceremony conducted on indigenous Mayan land. This was not a trendy approximation but a familial ceremony led by a traditional shaman and his apprentice at which I was a guest. As I experienced the ceremony, I naturally asked myself what I wanted in life—and what barriers I faced. I thought about how deeply fear dwells within me, as much as a physical organ itself, something noted on Day 5. Mind-body-emotional reactions are deeply conditioned into us—and often have physical or brain-chemical antecedents. What I am describing is not always easy to sort out. The body feels an emotion and the mind rushes in with a reason why. Yet the emotion is already present, perhaps resulting from an over-conditioned fight-or-flight response. Hence, the "reason" is often secondary. We tend to assign a reason after the fact of the emotion.

For all that, I also have responsibility for my repetitive returns to thoughts and figments aligned to fear. I cleave to certain patterns, people, or situations. Self-responsibility is undeniable. Rather than asking "why me?" the Mayan ceremony led me to ask: "What do I gain from this? Am I *enjoying my suffering*?" As alluded earlier, the seemingly self-defeating act of the same unhappy ritual must deliver some gain. My family member liked conflict. I came to accept that. For my part, I, too, like suffering or inner conflict. It provides a kind of visceral thrill.

I cannot imagine that my experience is entirely exceptional. None of us is as different from one another as we think. I ask you to search for the same pattern within. Do you enjoy your suffering? Is the greatest barrier you face to liberation—not the only but the greatest—the thrill or pleasure you experience from a sense of victimhood, danger, unhappiness, or hopelessness? These are not idle questions. This is your life.

I fully realize that circumstances are forced upon you that you do not choose, including parentage, health, physicality, geography, and socioeconomics. Where and in what circumstances you are born are a gravitational force. At the same time you also possess great latitude—which most of us constantly deny—regarding psychological choices and resources.

Take this day, Day 26, to face that in yourself.

It is often said—and I believe it's true—that no one would be drug or alcohol addicted if it weren't enjoyable. Intoxication relieves stress. It creates temporary feelings of enthusiasm, conviviality, and euphoria. Taken to mild excess, drugs and booze disrupt sleep patterns, promote lethargy and depression (which in turn requires higher doses), and eventually worsen everything they were ingested to escape. Chronically negative, conflictual, or violent emotional reactions *do the same thing*. They actually feel good and thrilling at first—catch yourself in this. Be watchful! But the resulting enjoyment, which may arrive as a sudden rush of satisfaction or rightness, soon devolves into depression, panic, or deeper shades of anxiety.

You must re-up the same "drug" to relieve the after-effects. This is what feeds caustic social media posts, for example.

If you can glimpse this even once in yourself, this day will open an entirely new door to you.

# YOU ARE NOT SOMEONE ELSE'S DECISION

N othing is more restrictive of your personal happiness than embracing values or decisions that belong to someone else but that you internalize and believe are your own.

We are often restricted by handed-down truisms that may not fit our individually experienced needs.

This dynamic occurs everywhere and in all ways. Hence, I am not going to complain about mainstream social mores, capitalism, advertising, body-image, or consumerist manipulation. That's not what you need to hear. If you are reading this book the likelihood is that you are already somewhat against-the-grain in your cultural and political attitudes. You are already rejecting of some of the so-called consumerist values of society.

My message to you today is that rejection of "mainstream" values, whether in appearance, economics, or social behaviors, *can be every bit as peer-driven and passive as the opposite*. Your peer group can, in its own way, be as restricting as anything that you grew up yearning to escape. Orthodoxy doesn't choose sides. It's always part of the human situation.

In that vein, let me ask you two questions: What is making you unhappy or unsatisfied—right now? And is it possible that there exists a solution or way out that is blocked by the values that you *think* you're supposed to be imbibing—*by someone else's decision*?

Has it occurred to you—and may the one-star reviews start flowing—that money, fashion, cosmetic surgery, a nice car, or some supposedly surface thing *may be the solution* for a situational problem that you are experiencing?

Solutions may, in fact, arrive in ways that are judged to be "superficial." (You'll recall this consideration from Day 8.) But superficial according to whom? Who is the person making that judgment and what is the content or state of his life and relationships that make him an authority on what is right or good for you or another?

Situational problems can be very serious. Solving one may not resolve your global issues. But anyone who thinks that money, for example, cannot solve problems either has too much of it or too little of it to know the difference. Anyone who thinks that worldly success cannot make you happy either has never experienced success or has spent his or her life chasing it, finding it, and would never give it up—despite holding forth on its limits. Bestselling social critic David Brooks proclaimed himself indifferent to learning that one of his books hit the bestseller list. Oh yeah? Would he sacrifice that watermark if he had the choice? I know a household name in the New Age field who grew enraged when his book, probably unfairly, was not included on *The New York Times* bestseller list. I don't judge him for it— although I do believe he ought to be transparent about such things in his teachings. When I got my first book offer from Random House I cried tears of joy. It was the culmination of years of effort. Don't draw conclusions about the value of success until you've occupied both sides of the equation.

I realize how easy it is to dispute what I'm saying. I know how fast and fully come the countervailing statements. "Be unattached to outcome." "You can't take it with you." "The outer fades, it's the inner that counts." The last was written to me by the conference organizer for a spiritual organization who objected to an article of mine about the spiritual dimensions of outer style. My interlocutor eventually acknowledged that he had not read the article. "I was responding to the picture and headline," he wrote. *That is exactly what is happening whenever people judge you.* They are reacting to what they think they see and, depending upon the cultural setting, how they believe spiritual or sensitive people are supposed to live. Sensitivity is never found in rote thought.

Your exercise for Day 27 is to claim liberty from judgments—including those you may have internalized—about the parameters within which your solutions or possibilities must fall. Whatever walk of life you're from, wherever you live, whatever your job, background, or cultural milieu: *you are free today to seek a solution that requires and receives no one else's approbation.*

Verify everything, including disallowed solutions, which may offer just what you need.

# DAY 28
## IS THIS NECESSARY?

admire the work of management guru Peter Drucker (1909–2005). In actuality, the business analyst was a deeply religious man whose work possessed greater dimensions than is sometimes understood. In my reading of Drucker's work, I find three core principles, which apply to both business and life in general:

1. Build on islands of strength and health.

2. Work only with people who are receptive to what you're trying to accomplish.

3. Work only on things that will make a great deal of difference if they succeed.

To this, I add a fourth principle:

 4. Always ask: Is this necessary?

This fourth principle has become more important in the digital age when we are presented with so
many chances—the word opportunities hardly seems
appropriate—to engage in frivolous behavior. The hive
mentality on social media encourages impulsive and
vituperative communication. But keep in mind that
when you act out randomly, emotionally, or to relieve
boredom (a special danger) you not only squander
your productivity but risk sullying your reputation
and damaging relationships. Other people are viewing and judging what you post—including coworkers,
employers, investors, and friends—who may be silent
but nonetheless note your behavior. Believe it or not,
a silent fraction of people do not abide by hateful language. And you may need them.

The founder of a publishing imprint for which I once
worked said about someone who sent us a superfluous
email: "He saw the opportunity to be a smartass and
he took it." We never viewed the person the same way
again. Do not allow that to be you. Starting today before
acting, speaking, posting, or communicating ask yourself: *Is this necessary?*

I once knew the media columnist for a high-flying but now-defunct publication whose star was clearly rising in the world. And he knew it. He had an appealingly sharp and clever writing style (provided you weren't on the wrong side of it), but he possessed a fatal flaw: he reveled in one-upping and insulting people. That trait used to be found in a segment of literary cocktail party goers who considered it a mark of high repartee. Yes, Oscar Wilde may have had a sharp tongue and Norman Mailer may have been pugnacious. If you're them, you can get away with it. But if you're not them, think very carefully about what I am writing. People remember every barb directed at them—and for a lot longer than the aggressor will. The media columnist I referenced? If I uttered his name today you wouldn't recognize it. In the end, no one stands by a smartass. They may temporarily fear or curry favor with such a person, but sooner or later the crowd thins and the blade falls.

The question of whether something is *necessary* follows us into every kind of situation, including busy work. I believe in meticulousness but not in superfluousness. Never engage in *task dumping*. Task dumping is burdening someone to do something for you before you've made the effort yourself. Or requiring something that

is unnecessary simply because you have the authority to do so, like sending someone to the back of the
line because he or she made a mistake on a form. Task
dumping is asking someone a question or to perform a
task because you can, not because it's necessary. It has
a spiteful dimension. In seventh grade I had a science
teacher named Mr. Marby who asked the class to fill out
a seating chart. If you messed up the order of the chart,
he said, you would have to rewrite the whole thing for
him as punishment (never mind the existence of eras-
ers). I messed it up. He followed me into my next class,
interrupted the class, and handed me his seating chart
to rewrite that night. It was morbidly embarrassing—
and a prime example of task dumping. (I discovered
that he actually wasn't such a bad guy. He had a fas-
cinating catalogue of knowledge about the Hindenburg
Disaster.)

During my publishing days an overzealous copyeditor was proofreading a final set of galleys. She
presented me with literally hundreds of last-minute
queries to send to the author. I refused. The writer was a
notable historian of stage magic; he was well-organized
and had done a thorough job. He had already passed
through several prior rounds of copyediting and proofreading. Beyond a few minor catches, the book was
finished. I would not burden a busy writer with a flood
of subjective, eleventh-hour queries from a copyeditor

whose judgment I questioned. I personally believe that copyediting has become a bloated and overstepping enterprise at many large publishers; it is due for reform. I did agree to send the writer a handful of queries that were absolutely objective, but not last-minute changes based on preference. I will not engage in task dumping.

One of the chief areas where we get habituated to non-necessity is superfluous talking. We as a culture have nearly lost our capacity for silence. We have stigmatized silence as indicating something wrong in relationships or unnatural when in proximity to others. Yet silence is wholly natural. We are not born talking but as soon as we learn the basic mechanisms of speech we are often induced to talk not out of necessity or for exchange of information or feelings, but at almost every instance. If you spend time around toddlers you will see how adults are always urging them to talk, often about frivolous things.

This habit follows us into adulthood where many people are unable to share a physical space, whether an elevator or airline row, without humming, complaining (watch especially for this), commenting on the weather, posing rhetorical questions, or drawing you into small talk. If you prefer silence they redouble their efforts. Resist this. Most talking is unnecessary and leads to needless entanglements with people who may have nothing to offer you.

Essayist Elbert Hubbard (1856–1915) wrote in 1912: "I believe that the greatest word in the English language is 'Sufficiency.'" Why the greatest? Because when we conserve ourselves we have sufficient amounts remaining to dedicate to what really matters. We benefit from these reserves, in energy, physicality, and reputatiion, when we avert the spillage caused from saying or doing too much.

# CHECK YOUR VALUES

reject the expression, "It's just business." *Nothing* is just business. As observed throughout this book: life is a whole. One act of dishonesty, fraud, or extortion is the same regardless of what playing field you tell yourself you're on. Remember Day 21?: *The way you do one thing is the way you do everything.* On this penultimate day I want you to run a check of your values—including those that are routinely neglected in our culture.

## LOYALTY

Isn't it odd how little we hear today about loyalty as a virtue? Yet in the primeval world, loyalty stood as one of the defining traits of life—loyalty to pack, tribe, family, friend, and community. Today the ideal is seen as quaint if not backwards. Many people upon hearing the term *loyalty* sniff something unhealthy in it and are apt to ask rhetorically, "Should I be loyal to a bad boss? A crook? A lousy friend?" No, you shouldn't. That would be an act of corruption. Loyalty is not groupthink or servility. Rather, it is reciprocity, reliability, and solidarity. You do not idly gossip about a friend. You do not avert your eyes from a colleague in trouble. You do not gloat, however subtly or insidiously, over someone's suffering. You do not accept summary or group judgments. If someone dwells within your circle of friends, workmates, or community (broadly defined), you start from a place of solidarity and protectiveness. You give succor so that person knows he or she is not abandoned when injured. You join someone's side. You'll need the same sooner than you think.

## SINCERITY

A teacher once warned me against being "stupidly sincere." He meant proffering a subjective opinion when not asked, which could cause injury or needless harm. I once knew a senior publishing executive who took pride in cutting down people's pretenses, or so she thought. What she often did was direct barbed comments at eager, earnest, and younger colleagues. She sent people home crying. When I finally called her out on it, the bully emotionally collapsed. She had been indulging in "stupid sincerity." Real sincerity means speaking the truth when asked, and doing so not at the expense of another, but of yourself. It also means speaking the truth wisely; as with my former colleague, harming another for no constructive purpose is not sincerity. Nor is withholding the truth always tantamount to lying. A lie implies malice; it means misleading someone for self-gain. Sincerity by nature is constructive.

## AESTHETIC INTEGRITY

One of the greatest exemplars of this trait was comic illustrator Steve Ditko (1927–2018). The co-creator of Spider-Man and Doctor Strange, and, in my view, one of the most innovative illustrators of the past century, Steve was notoriously private, intensely focused, and wholly dedicated to the integrity of his message and graphics. He would compromise on points of clarity but never on the core of his work. Some fans and colleagues believed he went too far in this regard. But I view Steve as heroic because he personally bore all of the consequences for his decisions. He reportedly turned down huge paydays for the Spider-Man and Doctor Strange movies because he didn't believe in their vision. That is the opposite of most commercially popular artists who complain all the way to the bank. I always tell people: "Don't be a hero after you cash the check." Decide what is and isn't worthy of compromise. I completed the full manuscript for my book *The Miracle Club* before submitting it to publishers. Some publishing houses wanted me to revise it, to make it more conventionally appealing. I refused. It was a complete vision, at least for me. I went with an editor who had the gumption to agree to those terms. Other times, compromise is entirely worthy. If you are paid by someone, you *do* owe them something—and that must be taken very seriously. Compromise—and even backing down (as explored on Day 2)— can be noble and productive. But you must compromise as a principled and considered choice. That is where aesthetic and artistic integrity reside.

## ACCOUNTABILITY

This is one of the more straightforward ethics—until you run into difficulty. Always take responsibility when things go askew. When a job is undone, finish it yourself. Consider yourself above no task. Never forget what it's like to clean a toilet. In fact, after a big victory, go home and clean your whole house, especially the gross parts. It keeps you grounded. I disdain seeing a boss ask an employee to do something that he wouldn't be willing to do himself, such as confront a difficult vendor or customer. In this sense, John Milton's Satan is a good manager. In *Paradise Lost*, when defeated and cast down to Hell, and facing perilous choices and tasks as to what to do next, Satan didn't send someone else to do his dirty work—he did it himself. Consider this passage from book two of Milton's epic. It is from the "Dread Emperor's" speech to his legions. I have rendered it into modern English:

> . . . *I should ill become this throne, oh peers,*
> *and this imperial sovereignty, adorned*
> *with splendor, armed with power, if anything proposed*
> *and judged of public moment in the shape*
> *of difficulty or danger could deter*
> *me from attempting. Wherefore do I assume*
> *these royalties, and not refuse to reign,*
> *refusing to accept as great a share*
> *of hazard as of honor, due alike*
> *to him who reigns, and so much to him due*
> *of hazard more as he above the rest*
> *high honored sits?*

## HONOR

This principle contains all the others—and something more. Honor means determining which relationships, roles, and personal encounters define you. And which you must fight against. I don't necessarily mean physically fight—though I do not discount that either—but I mean selecting those parameters of your persona that *cannot be violated*. This is a difficult principle to live by. As explored earlier, there is nothing wrong with a decision to back down. Every argument or instance of friction must be settled if a relationship or stability is to be maintained. When the path to intelligent compromise is not present, someone must back down. Sometimes the more powerful person selects that role. The key is that your decision must be a choice and not a psychological default. And what of physical conflict? That is a very personal decision. As noted, *The Art of War* counsels never to fight when you cannot win—this requires possessing a great deal of information about your foe. Other times, you may feel cornered and without a choice. I am not suggesting that you start a Fight Club; but I am suggesting that you know your surroundings, your capacities, and your limits—and decide what parameters you will accept.

## DIRECTNESS

Be plain and easily understood in writing and speech. Do not say something clever in an effort to insult or dominate another person—that's cowardly. If you believe something, and if it requires saying at all, then say it directly, clearly, and with ownership. Being a smartass is also a form of cowardice because you seek to dominate another person without really stating your position. Smartass remarks are endemic to online discourse, and they have intellectually and ethically eroded our culture. When called to speak plainly, most people (including intellectuals) are befuddled. Indirectness, bureaucratic language, hackneyed expressions, quips, wiseass remarks, and airs of mystery or inscrutability—all involve hiding. What you aren't willing to say plainly shouldn't be said at all. And what you aren't willing to say to someone's face—I'm speaking to you keyboard warriors—should not be spewed on social media. It is the ultimate act of hiding.

## TRUST

You must not only be reliable, but you must be *capable* of backing up your reliability with personal resources, agency, and aptitude. That facilitates trust. Do not make a "well intentioned" promise that you cannot keep. Pay your debts. Pay—and pay promptly—for services that you contract. I know a publisher who pays within 24 or 48 hours; it inspires tremendous loyalty—and trust. I know a prominent New Age center that makes a silent practice of breaking its commitment to pay its speakers, or at least those who aren't famous; the administration presumes that the speaker will "go away" and is happy to have spoken there as a resume builder. As soon as I detected that pattern I resolved never to work for that venue again. Trust is a stepping-stone to all other forms of power. If you cannot backup your intentions—which is the basis of trust—you can do nothing worthwhile. Possess the skills, means, and resources to allow people to invest their trust in you. If you do not have these things, do not represent their existence until you do.

## VALOR

This could also be called bravery, a term, like loyalty, that is now considered quaint or fanciful. Valor means pushing ahead toward great and necessary things, whether rescuing someone physically or emotionally; attaining an achievement against which all circum-stances are stacked; training your mind and body with intense discipline; or standing up for a principle know-ing that the consequences could cut for or against you. It means putting your name on something and willing to be known by what you attempt. Valor can be a small act, such as standing up to a bullying relative. It can be a large or public act of the kind you find in myth. Valor is not accidental, impulsive, self-indulgent, or thrill-oriented. It is purposeful. It is the ultimate act of agency. A single act of valor, when pursued from a place of principle and decisiveness, can change everything in your life.

## FORESIGHT

None of these ethics are valuable without foresight. Foresight means reflecting on the ultimate purpose and possible outcomes of what you're attempting. Your sense of self-determination must encompass gathering knowledge, pursuing education, consulting with authentic experts, and envisioning possibilities and alternatives. Bravery and daring, properly understood, are not reactions against boredom or ennui. They are mature and valorous expressions only when they are products of thinking, steadiness, and canniness. Know what you intend—and pursue it, whether success or failure results. The good news is that foresight also breeds persistency (or what some call faith) because it gives you new paths from which to approach a goal. Foresight is the prophecy of intellect.

Mainstream religionists, simply by associating with a certain doctrine or faith, sometimes feel entitled to the benefit of the doubt. By contrast, you ought to struggle internally and in your outer actions to earn your sense of personhood and rightness of expression. It is indeed a struggle—and that's the point. Struggle is the creative act. There can be no authentic ethics or selfhood without it.

# DAY 30
## ONE MISSING THING

I will not lie to you: I harbor a fervent and deeply felt wish for success on worldly terms. I have what I consider sound reasons for that. But I never allow my striving for audience, public notice, or money to compromise the nature of my search or my work, which are one and the same. We sometimes hear the term "selling out." Selling out means one thing: putting money before quality. That I will never do.

Nonetheless, I am driven in my wish for success and fame. I am being honest with you because I am asking you to be honest with yourself. I am revealing of things that don't always make me seem pious—I question the very concept—because we are trying to face and not escape from ourselves. And I do approach this book with the abiding conviction that "self," once discovered, does not necessarily require fixing. Ethical power reveals you to yourself.

That said, over the past year or so I have been gripped by a feeling that *something is missing* in my pursuit of success. I am failing to connect with some idea, approach, or principle. I have been unsparingly scrutinizing but unable to identify it. In the twenty-four hours preceding this writing, it came to me—unexpectedly and without my specifically looking.

Today, our final day, I want to share with you what I found in hopes that it may fill a vital need in your own efforts.

The day before writing these words I sat on a beach in Tulum, Mexico, watching local children walk up and down the shore attempting to sell trinkets, jewelry, and clothing to tourists. Like most tourists, I waved them away. Unlike some, my wave was generally accompanied by a smile and a "gracias, no." But that was that. I felt sorry for them but also told myself that I could purchase a hundred trinkets and it would make no difference socially. Was I right?

A little later that day, I noticed two couples lounging in the same area. They were Spanish-speaking tourists probably from Spain or Latin America. They were very chic and attractive. One of the men invited two beach kids, a girl and a younger boy, to eat from plates of food they had ordered at the hotel where we were staying. The boy seemed about nine years old but looked younger because he was small, probably because he didn't have much to eat in the way of healthy food. He gobbled down the chips and salsa like it was a rare and needed treat. One of the couples chatted with the girl, presumably his sister, who also ate. Why, I wondered, were these kids not in school? Who is profiting from their wares? A bit later another girl walked down the beach and they offered her a bottle of mineral water to drink from. When she went to return the bottle, they told her to keep it, and conversed with her a bit, too.

The world cannot be changed by buying some trinkets or offering food to a kid on the beach. But there is no question that that little boy and the girls had a better day, amid a very tough life, because of the kindness those people demonstrated.

I told my partner Jacqueline, "That's something I hardly ever do. I get too defensive." I am often too on guard to be kind in the ways that I should be in the world—in material, concrete ways that can make life a little easier for those who walk a very difficult road daily.

Later that night the experience returned to me. I was under the stars and I swore with totality of commitment—such an experience involves mind, emotions, and physicality—that my success must result in my intelligently and concretely assisting others. That, I realized, is the *missing thing*. That element had been absent as a consistently felt presence in my pursuit of success.

You may be thinking that I am a master at bursting through open doors. We often hear talk of "giving back." But I reject that principle as commonly expressed in the spiritual culture. That is because in most reaches of modern and alternative spirituality we are taught, however subtly, to reframe our wish for success as an act of covert altruism. This can produce a sweetly rendered but slightly insidious annunciation of our aims, as though we are disavowing ambition in favor of "Thy will be done." We attempt to sneak around a sense of burning drive—which requires no defense—as though it's all about others. Is it? Nothing productive ever comes from hiding. We are all creatures of attainment. Hence, I reject the claim of "service" uttered as an act of perfuming. And it is often so, however faintly.

I also realize that resources must be resolutely applied. I have neglected to think and act fully enough in terms of how I can do so on a broad scale, which is also part of reciprocity. I swore that I would use my success in this way. I ask you to do the same today. But only if it is sincere. Walk away and return to this step only if it feels real. Indeed, you may reject or alter what I describe in favor of a different missing ingredient. My only generalization is that one likely exists. You can determine it. If what I observe speaks to you, however, then allow it to be grounded by a starkly truthful principle uttered by a wise person: "The only things you can really give another person are time or money." Do not argue with that; live with it.

Author and therapist Piero Ferrucci told me a story from the life of British novelist and spiritual adventurer Aldous Huxley (1894–1963). Huxley had experimented with myriad tools of self-development, from psychedelics to projects in utopian living to various forms of Eastern spirituality. Huxley once met my hero Neville Goddard and couldn't fully appreciate what Neville was grasping for, but that influence was present, too. Toward the end of Huxley's life, the spiritual journeyer got asked by a reporter to name, among all the techniques he had explored, the best means for personal development. Rather than deliver some esoteric answer, Huxley replied: "Just try being a little kinder."

I realized on the beach that day that was my missing ingredient. It may be yours, too. If not, the question that it brings may lead you to something you have not previously realized was missing.

And that is the nature of the search that we are forever on together.

# APPENDIX
## *THE MIRACLE MONTH*
## READING GROUP GUIDE

Upon the initial publication of *The Miracle Month* in February 2021, I conducted a 30-day, online reading group in which we covered each day and its exercise. Included here are my short essays that accompanied our guided read. These selections can be used in a reading group or by a solitary individual as a companion to each of the 30 days in the book. I recommend reading these passages along with the concurrent exercise each morning.  —MH

## DAY 1: YOUR DAILY UNIFORM
Friends, Good morning. Welcome to the start of our 30-day reading club of *The Miracle Month*. If you have not

already, please begin by reading the introduction and Day 1 of the book.

The point of day one's "uniform" exercise is multi-faceted. First, it tells you who you really are. What we elect to wear—and elect to eliminate—is a private and powerful code. This code and choice assert your self-hood.

As I write in the chapter, adornment, as with every-thing in life, reflects the one whole that is you. Hence, if you alter one thing you alter everything, however subtly.

There is also a positive financial dimension to this act of paring down. I write this in *The Richest Man In Babylon Action Plan*:

> In terms of personal accouterments, it is far better to pay cash for one or two quality items, such as a Schott leather jacket or Chanel skirt, than a closet-ful of so-so items purchased on credit. A friend who studied fashion in Paris told me that one of her teachers would come to class each day wearing the same black Chanel skirt. At first, she thought it was weird. Then she realized the teacher was exempli-fying a principle. In Rome, the best cabdrivers wear designer suits. In many cases, it is the only suit they own. They always look great.

We live in an age of financial uncertainty. Resist the consumerist temptation to buy rather than make, temper, reuse, or reprocess. Later in the book, I write about the wonderful appearance of people who create a look versus purchase one.

I do not mean to dictate choices in the book. I list my own outerwear only because I want you to know that I mean what I write and I try to live by it. Also, you may have a job that requires certain choices, and that is wholly fine. The key thing is to be basic, self-determined, and integrative.

Simplicity, as I think you will see, is invested with a certain power. I believe that you will feel ebullient after making your uniform choices. And you will experience subtle changes stemming from those choices during our 30 days.

Begin now.

## DAY 2: GIVE IN

Friends, Good morning and welcome to Day 2 of *The Miracle Month*.

There are times in this book where I get hardcore and absolute—but before getting there we also must learn to bend and be flexible. One of the greatest ways of expressing this principle—and a way that will aid your psyche, time management, and stress levels—is to "give in." Today is the day to select one conflict—and surrender.

I learned long ago that there is no dishonor in giving in. In intractable conflicts, *someone* must eventually back down. Or the friction stretches on indeterminately and often destructively.

Now, as I write in the book: there are certain conflicts that must be faced down. Usually these are repetitive ones. Such as when someone is cruel to you as a matter of course. As you will see, I brook no compromise in such situations.

But circumstantial conflicts, matters of wounded pride, or even financial rip-offs sometimes just must be dropped.

Let me give you an example from my life that I did not include in the book. It played out just as I was finishing the book. I made the decision to accept an editing job, which I usually do not do. The contracting party abrogated the second half of our agreement. I walked away. The conflict simply would have proven too draining and would have inconvenienced mutual acquaintances. I took it on the chin. Dropped it.

Electing to drop a conflict is not about being wrong or about the other party being right. It is about realizing that you have greater horizons than victory in a given situation.

A colleague once asked me: "How much is your time worth to you?" Time is a tricky thing. *Emotions are time.* Freeing up emotional space is liberatory in ways that may not at first seem apparent.

In the corresponding chapter, you'll note that I tell a story of walking away from a financial tussle with my health-insurance carrier. Now, this is not always possible. It is not always advisable. But I made a strategic decision to give in to avoid stress and I allowed the system to win. I lost money. But a funny thing occurred. *The Kybalion* puts it this way: "Rhythm compensates." The sum returned to me in an unexpected way. This kind of thing *does* occur in life. There exist hidden tendrils of compensation. I consider this a natural law. Emerson wrote about it in his monumental 1841 essay "Compensation." Some call it karma. I call it cosmic reciprocity.

Hence, giving in—whether emotionally, financially, or contractually—can sometimes lay the way for a subtle victory. It can result in a relationship that might not have otherwise occurred. You might meet someone who experienced a similar thing and who is in a position to help you. You might gain justice in an unforeseen manner. And you will, very likely, feel a great deal better and more relaxed.

Losing is not really losing if there is self-agency behind it.

What I describe is not a universal recipe. But it is a powerful choice in selected situations. Choose one today.

## DAY 3: APOLOGIZE AND MEAN IT

Sincere apologies are transcendentally powerful. They realign reality. They are magick. They are alchemy. I write that because they create ripple effects that may extend beyond what is immediately or even ultimately knowable.

In the same manner that a seed planted will sprout in ways we do not foresee, so does a sincere apology alter nature.

But we withhold apologies. And apologies are withheld from us. I think this occurs because we believe that an apology concedes all responsibility for a hurtful act. But, as I attempt to express in today's exercise, apologizing to someone does not necessarily mean absolving that person of all contributing factors to a fractious situation. It simply means owning, acknowledging, and living up to my end of it. Without qualification.

As you will see later in the book—and you probably know by now—I do not take sentimental views of apologies or forgiveness. I question forgiveness. I am in no way certain that forgiveness or apology, for that matter, is right at every time and place.

But to be alive is to be involved in friction. All of us hurt people, knowingly or not. All of us have debts.

One rightly given apology pays a debt, at least to the extent that we are able. By "rightly given" I mean without condition.

Has anyone told you, "I'm sorry if you felt offended . . ." or "I'm sorry but . . ."? Such framings are worse than the original violation. Because they blame you for over-sensitivity or posit coequal blame. A fake apology injures twice.

Decide who is owed justice—and apologize sincerely during this 30-day period. It can be today. It can be next week. But it must be acted on. If the person to whom you are indebted cannot be reached—and hold yourself to a high standard: do not use this as avoidance—then you can tactilely write a letter to that person and save it.

I am not suggesting that an apology is something you do "for yourself." That is one of the bromides of popular spirituality. Rather, I believe in striving for reciprocity and debt payment and justice and honor. Primeval values. That is my effort, at least.

This month, we are powerful because we pay our debts. We live up to ourselves.

## DAY 4: BIKE EVERYWHERE POSSIBLE

Friends, This was a tough yet special section for me to write. I do not want to place untoward demands on people. I realize that a given physical activity is not right for everyone. But I did promise that this book calls for concrete and palpable life changes. Biking is one of them.

If you embrace biking as a way of life, you will discover a true personal difference.

You will feel better, stronger, and more able. You will be more relaxed. You will think of yourself differently.

When you bike, you not only encounter personal benefits that are foreseeable but ones *that are not foreseeable*. As I allude in this chapter, biking returns you to yourself in a manner that is wholly individualistic.

As I note in the book, if you have a physical challenge that makes biking impossible, please adjust this step to meet your needs. But act with agency and personal challenge.

This exercise does not need to be completed today. I realize there is expense involved, perhaps comparison shopping, and other needs. But begin. Especially if this step seems like a "pass."

At the end of these 30 days, let us circle back to this day as co-seekers. I ask you to review what you discovered and consider whether my claims proved valid and what they turned up for you.


## DAY 5: FACE YOUR ANGER

Friends, Welcome to Day 5. This is one of the most personal chapters I have ever written. I feel that I must be self-disclosing in this book because I am asking you to do the same.

I am only too aware of the theatrics displayed by many teachers, gurus, ministers, and even therapists. Having had an intimate view of the public life versus the private reality of many metaphysical thinkers, I never want to play into any kind of posturing, which is ultimately used to control people.

All of us react from anger. At its root, anger may be fear (that seems to me the case); but whatever its trigger, anger is one of the primary negative modes of expression in life—and it is expressed as punishment of another.

This may occur through overt intimidation, such as yelling, threats, or even physical violence; or it may be expressed perniciously through passion-aggression, such as withholding an obligation and then denying as much. Passive-aggression is anger mixed with plausible denial.

As I write in this chapter, I brook no fantasies about controlling emotions. Emotions run on their own track. They are faster than thought. This is why we often fail to express in a moment of emotion what we later wish we had said. Emotions are stronger than thought. This is why we break our mental vows. And emotions are more primeval than thought. Without healthful fear the individual would not survive. So, talk of controlling emotions is not part of my outlook.

But we can, with the right imperative, control the *unhealthful display* of emotions. This should not be overlooked. We are educated, perhaps miseducated, to believe that there must be unity between inner and outer life. E.g., "Let thine eye be single." That may be an ideal, but in humanity's general condition that ideal is as good as unattainable. It works only while seated in a chair.

My concern on Day 5 is with action. With relationships. With behavior toward another. And, if William James is correct (and some of the ancient religious sages agree with him), then the outer act itself will eventually come to shape the inner.

We can find impetus for the overt act by realizing the cost of anger. Weighing the cost pits one emotion against another. That is, I believe, a workable formula.

I do not specifically know why we imitate our parents. But it is a fact. We learn by example. My father displayed anger at home. I vowed never to do the same. Yet as the years creeped up on me, I looked back and realized that I had adopted at least some of his tonality. It is one of my great regrets in life.

Let this day serve to avert regrets.

At certain points in this book, I use seemingly harsh tones about human nature. To my thinking, you cannot possess real ideals without blunt reckoning. But I hope that I am as tough on myself as on another—and that the result helps facilitate an opening this month that makes us more reciprocal beings.

Power is not force. Power is generative. And it reproduces through relationships. Never see or use anger as power.

## DAY 6: STAND FOR SOMETHING

What does it really mean today to *stand for something*?

It does not mean tweeting or making cracks on social media.

It means risking some degree of calumny or even income to make a valued statement, defend a principle, or protect a colleague—when such an act is really critical minded, clarifying, and solidaristic.

I have been asked to turn my back on friends. I have refused. Loyalty matters. Loyalty is not corruption but rather the sustainment of solidarity when you believe someone deserves it. Regardless of what others think. And do bystanders know the situation?

I have been publicly kicked out of spiritual organizations or had talks canceled because of the controversial nature of my search. Like speech, a search that offends no one does not flex the boundaries of free expression. It is recitation and not exploration.

I do not ask you to court controversy. There is no intrinsic good in that. I do not try to court controversy.

I ask only that you speak so that others may speak. Seek justice, in whatever measure—including privately—so that others, too, may have justice.

One of the worst mistakes of my life was taking a job as a reporter at age 22 at a union-busting newspaper in Pennsylvania. It went squarely against my values. But I was eager to find work, I had to get out of my childhood home, and I permitted myself to be ruled by fear. I lasted 5 months before moving on. It was never the right fit. But, more importantly, taking that job subverted my values. I vowed that would never repeat. "Nothing can bring you peace," Emerson wrote, "but the triumph of principles."

I must emphasize: this day does not require some histrionic act. A private stand can be far more valorous (and risky) than a public one, especially when acting out in public has become a national pastime.

In *The Miracle Habits*, I wrote about the movie *Monsoon Wedding*. Let me reproduce that section here. It gets at the heart of our task for today:

A magnificent screen example of the power of recognition and acknowledgment of trauma appears in the 2001 Bollywood romantic comedy *Monsoon Wedding*.

Although I call the film a comedy it is much more than that. (Spoiler: I reveal the ending in this description.) The events unfold around a lavish wedding in Delhi, in which a modern Indian family is struggling with the expenses of marrying their daughter.

The householder Lalit is well off but nonetheless under financial strain as family from all over the world descend on his home and last-minute expenses pile up. Lalit and others glow with respect at the arrival of his wealthy, American-dwelling brother-in-law Tej, who has been a financial support to the family. One person, however, shrinks from Tej, Lalit's adult niece, Ria, who has lived with the family since the death of her father.

Ria soon notices Tej taking a flirtatious interest in a 10-year-old relative, Aliya. During an evening of pre-wedding festivities Ria spies Tej attempting to drive away with Aliya. She throws herself in front of the car to stop him and reveals the truth: Tej sexually abused Ria as a girl. Ria puts herself on the line to prevent this pattern from repeating.

Some family members accuse Ria of lying and say that as an unmarried woman she's just vindictive and bitter on the wedding eve. Lalit and his wife trust Ria, but their defense of her is muted and they are eager to avoid insulting the wealthy Tej. Ria flees the home. The following day, Lalit, still divided, pleads with Ria to return, which she does. Shortly before the wedding ceremony, the family is gathered before a small shrine to honor Ria's father. Lalit, in a moment of quiet but profound bravery, tells his benefactor Tej that he must leave their home. He stands up for Ria. As Tej departs, a tremendous burden is lifted from Ria—and 10-year-old Aliya is protected. The cycle has been broken. Ria is free. For me, it is one of the most subtly powerful and revealing moments in cinema.

If you want bravery, if you want to know what solidarity means, look at the characters of Lalit and Ria. They don't carry guns, wear costumes, or fly into battle—and they are some of the finest heroes that recent cinema has produced. Lalit cannot undo the past—or can he? The spiritual teacher G.I. Gurdjieff observed that the past controls the future, but the present controls the past. This can be understood on several levels. Here is one: the meaning ascribed to the past, and our response to it in the present, shapes the nature of the past.

Let people know who you are and what you stand for. Most importantly, let yourself know. That is our aim today.

## DAY 7: KEEP YOUR WORD

Many years ago, I published a book by a deeply intelligent and serious author who was part of a circle of neo-pagan and nature-based occult seekers in England. They held themselves to high standards. Their first principle: keep your word.

If you cannot keep your word, you can do nothing.

Nothing does more to strip away fantasies of "enlightenment," mawkish sharing of experiences, forced intimacies, self-idealization, anodyne prescriptions, or other habits of the alternative spiritual scene than the application of this one simple standard.

Striving to keep your word means sometimes failing. But to acknowledge that failure—and to feel it for real—is a help in itself. (Never use acknowledgment as evasion—a trick we too quickly learn. True acknowledgment involves suffering.)

In this book, I tell a story from the memoir *Boyhood with Gurdjieff*, a haunting and powerful record. I think I capture this episode accurately, at least insofar as the author related it. This is not easy. The spiritual teacher Gurdjieff cannot be readily summarized in his lessons or in any of the episodes surrounding his life. People often attempt to compare Gurdjieff's ideas or methods to other things or to restate them: "Oh, it's like . . ." A philosopher friend of mine used to say, "It's not *like* anything."

I note this to come around to a related point. The greatest benefit I personally received from the Gurdjieff work was the stripping away of fantasies.

We in the modern West are suffused with contradictions. In one of those contradictions, we are taught again and again—corporately, educationally, therapeutically, and spiritually—how special we are. People are filled with puffed up views of themselves. They are also filled with the opposite—we receive confounding messages. We are often told we are special so we can be sold things. New Age culture, which does many good things, also encourages this "I'm special" attitude. But get assigned a difficult and unfamiliar task at an inconvenient hour and you will see how powerful or special we are. Generally, not very.

Keeping your word is a way of measuring yourself. It reveals your relationships and how others experience you. Alcoholics Anonymous co-founder Bill Wilson made the important observation that progress is measured *by others*—they see us first and most clearly. How others see and experience you rests heavily on the extent to which you keep your word.

Today's effort is simple. Simple in the sense of basic. But it goes to the heart of who we are.

Keeping your word requires eschewing some familiar comfort. If done sincerely, keeping your word becomes a source of power because it strips away theatrics and delusion and leaves standing the being who you truly are. That being possesses an extra-physical existence. That being possesses a psyche. And that, I believe, is where actual power resides.

# DAY 8: WHAT DO YOU WANT?

Friends, As I was preparing today's post, I was reminded of one of my favorite quotes from Friedrich Nietzsche: "Formula for our happiness: a Yes, a No, a straight line, a goal."

This is from Walter Kaufmann's translation of Nietzsche's *The Antichrist*, written in 1888 but considered sufficiently controversial so that its initial publication was delayed until 1895. It was not bluster when Nietzsche wrote in his preface, "Only the day after tomorrow belongs to me."

Many of us are educated to think of "serious" philosophy as scholastic, logical, macro, and abstract. I dissent from that. Philosophy should govern next Tuesday.

In an 1898 lecture, William James challenged American philosophers to produce a philosophy of "*cash-value*, in terms of particular experience," with his emphasis in the original. Ralph Waldo Emerson wrote essays on the themes of "Wealth" and "Power," speaking of such things not abstractly but explicitly. We need a philosophy of actuality. Of results. One that honors the goals of the individual rather than seeking to deny, rearrange, or ignore them.

*What do you want?* That be the most important question of your life. It belongs to you alone. It has no parameters.

I believe that nothing does more to enact the powers of the psyche—including the causative and creative potentials of thought—than focusing on one passionately felt aim. It is the single greatest guarantee we have of getting where we wish to go. It is not an absolute guarantee. But it is the closest that we are granted.

Why the emphasis on focus? Nature is powerful when focused. Air, water, light—all are dispersible. But when concentrated, all are extremely powerful. We mirror nature. "As above, so below." Focus is extraordinarily powerful.

In today's passage, I ask that you state (privately) exactly what you want. You may or may not be able to attain it in the precise mind-eye's form it takes. Life often delivers things to us in disguise. But to not know is a tragedy. And we often do not know because we internalize peer pressure in ways that deter self-acknowledgment. As self-indulgent as our culture is, peer pressure and conventions of self-image often deprive us of the bravery to be internally honest.

Allow today to be a day of total freedom within—acknowledge what you want; be specific; write it down; tell no one. This is the seed of attainment. You will receive something.

## DAY 9: UNDERSTAND POWER

This was one of the toughest chapters in this book to write. I ask myself: Did I go too far? Was I too harsh? Overly judgmental?

Having true ideals means facing the realities of human nature. One of the tough truths that I had to learn (and am still learning) is that most people rarely act from principle or excellence but from momentary gain or a narrow range of presumed benefits.

My belief is: the response to ignobility is not more ignobility. It is principled resistance. It is clear vision. It is truth-telling. *The 48 Laws of Power* and its lessons on how to manipulate people or events is not my antidote. I actually find *The Art of War* and even Machiavelli's *The Prince* more idealistic. I recommend reading both (a point to which we return in these 30 days).

One might ask: *why not* stoop to the level of those who wield power crassly? I do not have any dramatic response to that. I suppose that within my psyche I believe in reciprocity and some measure of personal honor. My heart will never be with Brutus. If you are reading these words, I would warrant that you are probably somewhat similar. We cannot act effectively if we act against our natures.

Let me share a personal detail. I wrote this chapter in July of 2020 after a media giant failed to pay me scheduled royalties and ignored my emails eight weeks after the matter. Those of you who are contractors, consultants, artists, or freelancers know the predicament. You are put into a vise grip of having to be "polite" in order to secure (presumed) future business while tolerating unethical behavior. It puts a person in front of the very questions that this chapter explores. (On a happy note, I did finally get paid and fixed the problem. Maybe due to the methods we explore today. Although why things change is not always clear.)

In short, a person can never be powerful in the world of materiality unless he or she acknowledges—without necessarily bowing to—the tools of power.

Many of us face questions around the conditions under which to provide or withhold our labor. When confronting such issues, think over them carefully. What do you owe to expediency? What do you owe to principle? There are no off-the-shelf answers.

I have three general rules in matters of power:

1. Tell the truth.
2. Never work twice for a dishonest dealer. (This can be difficult in our world.)
3. Value what you have to offer; people come to you not because you are like them but because you provide them with something that they believe they need. They may be right.

Reflect today on how you have dealt with issues of power—or agency of self—in the temporal world. How have you gotten things done in a world where honor, reciprocity, loyalty, and excellence are too rarely cultivated? Let us search together.

## DAY 10: MAKE THE ASK

What does it mean to ask for what you want in life?

One part of it—perhaps the most important—is deserving it. This means earning it.

Years ago, an artist on the Lower East Side of Manhattan created a robot that exploded and spewed out little strips of paper with expressions on them like: "Demand undeserved rewards." We must live up to our asks.

But for some of us—and I find myself in this category, which you may be, too—making the ask is difficult. We fear loss. Hence, we aim—and ask—too low.

Apropos of yesterday's exercise, asking is a form of power. It can come in the positive or in the negative. An ask can reflect what we won't accept. If a client, venue, neighbor, or partner offers something below what we consider appropriate, refusing is a healthful act. Refusing can also beget receiving. It "clears the decks" in ways that are both material and unseen. One of the principles of this book is that these realms are one and the same.

I opened today's chapter with an observation from Cardi B. I would now like to add another from a different musician whose work I grew up with: Joe Jackson. One of his songs is titled: "You Can't Get What You Want Till You Know What You Want." Do you? What role does money play in your life? Peer recognition? Independence?

The responses belong to you alone. Once you are frank with yourself, you will have an easier time making asks.

Before these 30 days are up—and 20 remain—I want all of us to make a major ask. Begin today. Make a decision. Work toward it. Act on it.

## DAY 11: F COLLEGE

As I write these words, the Covid pandemic has forced many unwelcome changes on us. It has impelled shifts in our economy, many of which are burdensome to workers, including long-term arrangements to pay for your own at-home workspace, upkeep, tech, and utilities.

But it has also given us a chance to rethink the manner in which higher education is structured and financed. Will we take it?

I ask you to use this day to think seriously about the nature of training and education that are necessary in your life—and in the lives of those you love—and, ultimately, about the nature of work itself.

I have long felt that our culture devalues the trade professions (e.g., carpentry, contracting, electrical work, plumbing, and so on), without which we could not function. I am leery of the vast number of college degrees that prepare the graduate for almost no work in life.

I secured a job before I left college—in April, in fact, when my graduation was in June. I had no choice but to work. It was harrowing but also helpful. Nothing focuses the mind like necessity.

But I am concerned that we are raising generations of students with massive debt loads and degrees that may or may not be wholly useful in the world.

For a time, I was involved with an accredited distance-learning college. I realized that state accreditation—which requires paying large fees to accrediting agencies—was so important to the administration because it allowed students to apply for student loans. That was the business model of the school. But I questioned whether the degrees granted were of much good to the veterans, homemakers, and seekers who were taking on debt to obtain them.

I realize that college degrees are necessary in certain areas of employment. Certification, licensing, and qualifications for the professions and sciences are obviously critical, at least if one wants to pursue a traditional career path.

But, beyond that, I really ask you to think flexibly about higher education. And think about what peer pressure and social culture tell us are "good" jobs. My oft repeated statement to my kids: "You can be a plumber who loves opera, can't you?"

During the Great Recession of 2008, I knew a financier who got laid off from his bank. He had carpentry skills. He took up a new job—and a new lifestyle—by working as a carpenter on movie sets. He *glowed* under the experience. Now, I am not blind to the fact that he also had connections: getting a union card as a carpenter in New York City is in an inside job. It is not always fair. That aside, this former financier discovered a fortifying, enjoyable, and well-paying new career—and new life—by working with his hands.

Likewise, I know the owner of a successful children's hair salon in Brooklyn who was pursuing a higher-ed degree in child development. See eventually realized that not only did she love cutting hair (and proved great at it) but there was a component of education and childcare in her work, since she cut the hair of very young kids with whom she had a "magic touch." Her appointment calendar is packed.

I am not prescribing one way of life for another. I am not idealizing trades, crafts, or labor versus office or cultural work. I also know Teamsters who are unhappy in their jobs. And I realize, and have previously bowed to, the pressures of taking corporate work for health insurance. But I ask you to think flexibly about what you do in education and work. We have limited control over so many decisions. Where you elect to spend your educational dollars—or those for someone you love—is among those few decisions. And it can impact someone for the rest of his or her life.

Take this day to carefully review education options, purpose, and prospects.

## DAY 12: FIND THE SCISSORS YOURSELF

Today's step is, in a sense, a return to basics: *do for self in small things.*

It is simple. It is graspable. It is achievable.

But there is a greater dimension, as with every seemingly small step.

Imagine the changes that could ripple through your life, your self-image, and your relationships if you internalized the principle at the heart of this chapter: overdependency on others erodes your sense of self-respect as it also erodes your basic abilities and acumen.

I recently caught myself slipping into a minor pattern of dependency in matters of cooking, food prep, and meal planning. I saw the effects accumulating and vowed to reverse course. Doing so strengthened my relationships and household. It rippled through several areas of my life.

Relationships, careers, and households often experience turning points over seemingly small things. Anything that becomes a repository, symbol, or fulcrum for *emotion* dramatically touches your surrounding environment. This fulcrum can be as small as routinely making or leaving a bed unmade. How does it affect people around you?

I believe that a small commitment, made passionately and lived by (even if fitfully) can change your world. Even the world. Imagine if just 10 percent of the public, or even 1 percent, took this vow—and meant it:

> I *will first make every effort to meet my own needs before requesting assistance from another;* I *will enlist another's help only when matters of personal wellbeing or safety are involved or I have made every reasonable effort on my own.*

We harbor enormous resentment of others—*and subtle shame of self*—over matters of superfluous dependency. Let us, for our own part, disrupt that cycle today.

# DAY 13: GIVE UP ONE THING THAT CAUSES YOU PAIN

I hope that there are periods during our time together when you encounter a section that speaks exactly to what you need at a given moment.

That occurred for me the morning of this writing.

I do not recall the order in which I wrote each of my chapters in this book. I reread each day's chapter in the morning before writing its companion piece. I did not write these supplementary passages in advance. I wrote them in real time as I was also performing each exercise, each day. In that sense, I am doing the exercises with you day by day.

I had been experiencing difficulty with a business vendor. I woke up and did a Tarot card reading about the matter. It stunk. I told myself: I am either going to hang onto this unproductive relationship or cut the cord. I could not fathom the vendor's behavior, but that's the choice I faced.

I then reencountered this chapter.

We must acclimate ourselves to getting rid of draining, disruptive, or unproductive attachments. We cling to these things before *we fear the loss of the familiar; we fear that it cannot be replaced.* But the result is that we cling to an empty (or even poisoned) urn, hoping that it will flow with fresh water once again, rather than smashing the urn on the rocks, or just leaving it on the roadside and searching for something new. A statistician once told me: "Life favors action."

The meaning of today's exercise is not in whether you give up something large or small. It is that you give up *something* in order to prove to yourself that it *can be done*. That the sun rises tomorrow. And probably a better sun, filled with the sustaining powers of self-respect and new beginnings.

I ask you this day to give up something really identifiable, personal, possibly material. It is your choice. And remember, whatever you do on a micro scale can be repeated on a macro scale. That is the promise of seemingly small step.

## DAY 14: ACKNOWLEDGE THAT YOU DO NOT KNOW

Those of you who have been reading me for a while know that I often inveigh against gossip. This is not some goody-goody ethic. The fact is: we know next to nothing about the lives we routinely discuss—and debase.

This came home to me recently when I learned a host of surrounding details about an artist who was accused of committing an act of violence. The surrounding factors were very complex. But the people who were lined up to repeat stories and throw stones knew (and cared) little about the variegated issues involved.

The antidote to this and related situations is not necessarily "more information"—how great can our info intake finally be?—but rather suspension of certainty and lowering of zeal to repeat and to judge.

There are situations in life in which all of us are called to make judgments or identify injustice or to protect self or others. I am in no way counseling indifference. But those acts will be greater, fuller, and more serious when we raise the bar of personal standards by which we make decisions.

The question of how we judge, and of which sources we trust, colors so many facets of life. Especially controversial issues. I realize that gun owners know things about firearms and gun-control policy that I do not. They have outlooks on gun ownership that are more personal and, in many cases, better informed than my own. This does not mean that my points of view are wrong but they may be incomplete.

On a different tack, I am struck by the repetitive arguments used by hardened skeptics of ESP research and psi phenomena. They routinely offer that there isn't a "shred of evidence" for the existence of ESP. They authentically believe this. This is an emotional conviction as impervious to alteration by countering facts as the most deeply held religious certainty.* It is an attitude reflective of general human nature.

A lot of opinions grow out of whatever makes us feel powerful or safe. We often feel powerful when throwing a stone. We feel safe when disabling a point of view that summons a pang of fear in us. These emotional factors do not mean that we are mistaken or wrong. But we can all take steps away from easily reached or endlessly repeated certainties.

Many of us bemoan the poor state of online culture. Much of it is sarcastic, coarse, frivolous, and know-it-all. It can seem as though no opportunity to be a smart ass is left untaken. Escalating comments are the norm.

What to do? Improve the culture within. You become stronger and a beacon to others.

As suggested earlier, a change among a small fraction of people or even a change in one person can ripple in ways that we may be not foresee.

## DAY 15: RECONSIDER FORGIVENESS

This chapter brings us to the midstream of our 30 days. My approach in this chapter is twofold:

---

\* A comprehensive meta-analysis of psychical research data appeared in the flagship journal of the American Psychological Association: "The Experimental Evidence for Parapsychological Phenomena: A Review" by Etzel Cardeña, *American Psychologist*, 2018, Vol. 73, No. 5, 663–677.

1. I truly believe that in order for a search to be real, seekers must—subjecting no one but themselves to their experiments—verify all spiritual and ethical principles that are handed down to us.

2. I invite you to question whether the presumed imperative of forgiveness speaks to the necessities of every life and situation.


"You've got to forgive to live." "To err is human, to forgive, divine." "You don't forgive for another, but for yourself." We are surrounded by injunctions to forgiveness. It is a truism within the cultures of spirituality and recovery. I am not cynical on the matter. I am not rejecting of it. But I am *questioning*.

I had a family member who behaved in persistently destructive ways, reveling in argument, provocation, and the triggering of emotional duress. She gaslighted. She broke her word. She took from others and abandoned them when they got sick or hit hard times.

I tried to speak with her about this—for years. I tried to counsel her as best I could that the brevity of life is such that these behaviors couldn't sow good fruit for long. My pleas were ignored.

A therapist once asked me, "Look, do you think she did her best?" My response: "No."

Should I forgive this person? Well, it's an open question. I tried to for years. I have worked with Richard

Smoley's brilliant book, *The Deal*—the finest spiritual argument for forgiveness that I know. You might want to read it hand in hand with this chapter.

In the case I just described, with there being no evidence of countervailing behaviors up to the end of this person's life, I found the question of forgiveness irrelevant, forced, and unnecessary to charting a constructive arrangement and memory.

For me, a better way has been using that life as a cautionary model of what I do not want to do myself. The anger that I feel sometimes swells up and then recedes based on the passage of time and on changes brought about by the life process and its eventual physical end.

*Live not this way* is my redeeming lesson. That, and not forgiveness, is my restorative principle.

Should victims forgive their attackers or tormentors? I am not sure. In some cases, where it is constructive and helpful to the victim—and where honesty prevails—I would probably defend whatever act an injured party finds ethically restorative, *provided it does not surpass the violative nature of the offense.*

I am not against forgiveness. I am against orthodoxy.

I have attempted to work with *A Course In Miracles.* Its entire basis is forgiveness. It is a brilliant work. But it is not my path. Contrary to the *Course,* I do not believe that human striving is illusory. I do not believe that love—an amorphous and overused word—is necessarily the epicenter of life. I believe that the strive to create is the epicenter of life.

Consider your experiences with forgiveness, positive, negative, and yet unfolding. Let us search together.

## DAY 16: ESCAPE CRUELTY

Friends, since I am doing this month in real time with you, I do not, as noted, always recall the chapter that is directly ahead. I was surprised, as you may have been, that today's passage reflects back on some of the issues we considered yesterday.

I realize that I sometimes adopt a take-no-prisoners tone in this chapter, and I hope that it does not go too far. My wish is not to be condemnatory but liberating. While growing up, we are rarely taught that we possess the option of cutting ties with cruel people. Unless, of course, we are bound to them domestically or economically; but even then, we are rarely encouraged to think in terms of immediate or imminent separation.

I recall a woman on social media telling me that her mother tormented her at every opportunity. She described bullying, cut downs, and so on. Her mother had recently died. She did not, she wrote, regret the woman's passing for a moment and was happy to be free. To be frank, I honor that woman.

The conventional wisdom of our therapeutic culture—a culture that I also honor because it grants us language and insights unavailable to past generations—says that my correspondent is harboring emotional repression and must come to terms with the feelings that she is denying in the wake of her mother's death. I am not so sure. I believe that sensitive people are capable of stating their needs and feelings, and sometimes those things are plainly situational. Getting away from a tormentor is almost always liberatory in remarkable and unseen ways.

The day before writing these words, I visited a newly opened barbershop in Williamsburg, Brooklyn. The owner-operator told me that he opened the place during the first summer of the Covid lockdown. He did his research and felt that he could make it work. He was right. But he added that he was also cautious about telling his friends or peers what he was doing. He did not want to invite unsolicited doubts, judgments, or putdowns about opening a business during a time of crisis.

I found his story moving and insightful. Again, he did his research—he crunched the numbers, had savings, and was well prepared. He fully understood the challenges from the lockdown. This was not some off-the-handle venture. But he also realized that uninformed peers and friends could sow doubts, which would weaken his resolve. This is the world we live in. Passive hostility is common to the human situation—and requires navigating.

I wrote "hostility" and not fear or negativity because I think that is the truth. I was inspired in this regard by spiritual teacher Vernon Howard (1918–1992). Vernon considered hostility the core human problem. And he believed that you should never be required to tolerate it, or its byproduct: cruelty.

If someone is cruel to you—and you know it when you experience it—cut that person off today. It could be an online acquaintance. It could be a presumed friend. It could be someone more consequential in your life. If the latter is the case, and if you cannot physically escape right now, consider what this chapter offers in the way of a two-step process.

I hope this proves one of the best days of your life.


## DAY 17: WRITE A BIO

Friends, I realize that today is a departure from some of our more psychologically themed exercises—but I believe that in a short time you will find this effort a useful and propitious undertaking.

We are often shy or uncertain about telling the world who we are. And yet we are, sometimes at unexpected moments, called upon to do so.

Once you have written a basic statement of self, you will have a clarified sense of how you want to announce yourself. You will have meaningful responses to job interviewers, event planners, customers, clients—and yourself.

We spend more of our lives working than we do among loved ones. That is just a fact. To neglect or downplay that area of life is to downplay the waking hours of your existence. Honor the working facet of your life by knowing who you are professionally. Be clear, specific, honest, and bold.

You may find yourself in the surprising position of needing such a document before the end of these 30 days or soon thereafter. You will also have a clarified sense of what you want to get across about your work and abilities.

You will not likely complete such a document today. But begin drafting it. Aim to complete it, or a serviceable version of within 2–3 weeks. Begin now. You will be glad you did.

## DAY 18: WIN NOBLY

This was one of the most meaningful chapters for me to write. I reiterate its principles in the "landmark edition" of *The Art of War*, which I annotate and introduce along with a translation of the *Tao Te Ching* by sinologist Lionel Giles.

I wonder if what I write in this chapter is serviceable on the field of life?

It is not a formula for victory *at any cost*. It is a formula for victory with honor. Is that quaint? I do not ask that rhetorically. I wrestle with that question.

Having worked for more than twenty-five years in corporate publishing, I witnessed a lot of people come and go. It seems to me, and I write this somberly, that some of those who lasted the longest survived based not on the quality of their work but on their capacity to identify and serve the bureaucracy. Hence, it mattered little if their output was mediocre; they identified the right people whom not to offend and pursued that as their primary job. I am sure this is true in most corporate workplaces, as well in the military, NGOs, academia, and so on.

I have known my own episodes of success and failure—by which I mean conduct and attainment—and I feel certain that life is whole. Hence, I do not believe in the expression "it's just business." What could that possibly mean? What you do is who you are.

I do not know—and I write this with deepest seriousness—whether I am helping you in the direction of career advancement or other immediate goals within this chapter. The point of this book is to bring you ethical power; I want every passage to prove useful. But I also believe that we need men and women who do their best to tell the truth; who will not fudge numbers to make a product or themselves "look good;" who do not impugn the character of another person for cheap gain; and who will not call spoiled food fresh based on contingency.

At the same time, I also want you to prevail, to gain, to win—in those areas where your attainment is earned and in the natural order of things. This often requires training, excellence, watchfulness, and decisiveness. It means the willingness to withhold your labor. It sometimes means taking the longer road.

I have known bosses, as I am sure you have, who had a talent for being out of the room whenever a crisis arose; who always managed to be out of sight or otherwise committed when a fire needed putting out; who managed to get other people's fingerprints, rather than their own, on troublesome projects. I have seen such behaviors rewarded. But that is not our approach today. Ours is winning nobly—in a manner that serves your psyche and self and not just contingency. That's the only leadership I consider real.

Am I right? Consider this today from the laboratory of personal experience.

## DAY 19: EMPATHY VERSUS SPITE

I believe that life is composed of polarities—every event, every emotion, every deficiency is complemented and compensated by some variant of its opposite. Life is rhythmical and compensatory, often in unexpected ways and not necessarily on a discernible timetable.

We can learn a lot about ourselves by locating our emotions and actions on the sliding scale of a polarity. Hence, in evaluating how we behave toward others (and self) I challenge us today to really ask where we fall on the empathy-spite continuum. And do so with steely eyed realism.

I have been self-disclosing in this chapter because I ask the same of you.

We all consider ourselves "good." Everyone who throws a rock at another believes that he or she is doing so in the name of peace, justice, and rightness. People who make caustic comments on social media believe they are correcting wrongs or delivering a message of refreshing truth. They believe that they are admired for it.

Hence, evaluating our actions in the light of "justice" can be self-deceiving. All of us have suffered. We all feel owed something. We all think of ourselves as creditors rather than debtors. But on an intimate scale, we often exact prices from people who did us no harm and who were not present when an inceptive harm was committed.

What's more—and this is one of the most pernicious aspects of human nature—we often take a prurient thrill from violence, whether verbal or spectacle, whether self-committed or witnessed.

I have seen people who consider themselves victims talk about their injuries in ways that are ultimately intended to harm the listener, such running down a joint project. That is an act of bullying. It is concealed violence, sanitized through claims of victimhood.

To feel an excess of debt owed you usually betrays a lack of empathy. The person who defrauded or mistreated us (such as a parent, teacher, sibling, or peer) may not be on the scene or accessible, so we take the debt from the skin of another person, often in subtle ways. This is why cries of victimhood often conceal aggression. One thing that every aggressor has in common is a feeling of rightness.

We often avoid meaningful questions of good and evil by framing them in macro terms, asking where we or another fall on some ultimate scale. (This is the "Hitler equation" that always emerges in online disputes.) But we live in world of quotidian events and intimacies. Relationships and households often stand or fall based on seemingly small episodes, which, as alluded earlier, are fulcrums of emotion.

Today, we break this blinkering cycle or at least disrupt it. We ask across life and at this hour: *where do I fall the scale of empathy versus spite?*

This does not mean abnegating yourself. This does not mean saying yes when you mean no. Those are your decisions. But make them as decisions and not as defaults. Know where you stand. And where you wish to stand.

## DAY 20: THE POWER OF RESPECT

This is one of the longest chapters in the book—and the one with the greatest potential for immediate payoff.

In terms of career, commerce, legalities, street life, confrontations, social media, and relationships of every kind, the practice of respect can change everything for you.

I have been working with these principles most recently on social media. With the lockdown (and even without it) we spend most of our waking lives in cyberspace. We dwell there among strangers—including those who are disputatious, cynical, and often anonymous—more than among loved ones. Consider that for a moment.

It is critical to regularly check your actions on social media. Are you participating in escalating and meaningless posts? We revisit that issue and its implications later in these 30 days. But let me offer a few observations now about online life.

It is astounding and alarming to observe the extent to which sarcasm, insult, exaggeration, taunt, and simple cruelty abound online. Human nature has not changed with the advent of the digital age.

But the social remove of anonymity, the algorithmic prioritization of contentious posts, and the apparent (and illusory) lack of consequence have put us at one another's throats.

I told my older son, who was 16 at this writing: "Your generation is going to have to fix this. If we as a nation do not eschew hateful and escalatory communication online, we will not make it."

He is abler than I am. Three or four years ago he cautioned me against getting into political squabbles online. I am finally listening. I post virtually nothing about politics today. It is not that I lack commitments. Nor am I urging everyone to follow my practice. (Journalists and commentators have their jobs, too.) But casual posting about politics causes fights while *changing virtually nothing*. In fact, such posting may worsen things because it is *ersatz action*. It is vanity to believe that I am "taking a stand" in a tweet or post.

Demeaning people over social media, politically or otherwise, returns to haunt you. For one thing, I do not see how anyone posting bile from behind the screen of anonymity can maintain self-respect. It is cowardice. Unless a vital misunderstanding is at stake, I almost never reply to anonymous confrontation on social media.

People read and take seriously what you post online—a fact that may at first seem thrilling but later can become complicating or compromising. A social science professor who is a critic of New Age once posted that he saw me as having "done humanity great harm" because of my popularization of occult and New Age books and ideas. He went on to make a few more related remarks. He then blocked me so I could not reply. I wasn't planning to. The same person later came back around wanting to dialogue, but the sense of constructive relationship and my once-positive estimation of him was ended.

In addition to aimless stone-throwing, we must also curb our routine use of sarcasm, eye rolls, rhetorical questions, and gibes. When someone posts a denigrating aside, whatever the supposed issue, that person is engaging in hostility. Plain and simple. It is difficult to resist responding to a gibe. But resist it all the more, as you would the needle or the bottle if you were in recovery. Do I exaggerate the stakes? Decide for yourself at the end of this passage.

Small case in point. Several years ago, I posted an article at Medium about the French mind theorist Emile Coué (1857–1926) who I greatly admire. Coué popularized the use of affirmations, including his famous, "Day by day, in every way, I am getting better and better;" he pioneered the method of conscious autosuggestion; and he foresaw some of today's advances in placebo studies. Culturally, Coué was an influence on The Beatles who quote him in some of their songs. The evening prior to my writing this passage (synchronicity?) someone posted the remark: "I suggest that you Google toxic positivity." Of course, my first impulse was to write back in a similar tone, "I suggest that you . . ." Now, for years I have written critically about positive-mind metaphysics; I considered attaching an exculpatory link. But . . . I did nothing. No one likes to feel misunderstood. And social media almost always feels personal. Its tech is designed that way. But *we simply must put an end to perpetual contest online*. We cannot turn every exchange in one-upmanship.

Do not over-analyze algorithms, complain about the evil, hoodie-wearing Zuck, or wait for anti-trust legislation. Decide unilaterally to exit online bickering. Stop. Desist. It is in your power. Such an act will positively redound to you both personally and socially. To start with, it lowers stress and increases discretionary time. More importantly, you will experience greater self-respect.

One final note about respect online. The "unfollow" is often used as a passive-aggressive weapon particular to our age. When someone angers or disappoints you, the impulse to unfollow that person quickly arises. Such an act can feel like an immediate release. It can, so we believe, "teach them a lesson." A rule of thumb: wait six months. Unfollows hurt people. They send a message, and perhaps not the one you intend.

I have helped people get books published only to notice one day that they unfollowed me. Did I venture an opinion they disliked? Overlook an email? Withhold some expected support? I do not know. But the act always strikes me as petty. That said, I am guilty of it myself. I have vowed not to unfollow people out of emotional disdain and not to reciprocate when I am unfollowed that way.

Adolescents are reduced to anguish by unfollows. Adults are too. Unfollows can be a grotesque, or at least grotesquely abused, feature of social media. It falls to the individual to correct.

I have spent most today's passage dealing with social media because that is where we primarily "live," especially right now. I have recently pondered: what is the role of the social rebel within a digital culture that is coarse, degrading, and petty? Be that rebel.

I have not succeeded at everything I write here. I experience lapses. But together and as individuals, practicing online respect is one of the most radical steps we can take.

## DAY 21: ONE THING DONE RIGHT

It is not always possible to be meticulous with every task or to be aware of how another person experiences your work, efforts, or behavior. But I do believe that to really do something means doing it wholly and right. To perform a task in a less than whole manner burdens another person and reduces his or her experience.

As I write this passage, I am dealing with a vendor who has pulled a "no show." He had a deadline for today. He was paid and communicated with in timely manner. Yet for several days he has ignored (or so I gather) emails from a colleague and me. No response. No status update. No delivery.

I am, to be frank, at a loss for such behavior. I used to witness it in publishing, too, where a writer on deadline would sometimes "go silent" and prove unreachable. In all my years as a fitful student of human nature, I could never understand how someone could consider such a response appropriate or within bounds of acceptable behavior.

At the very least, let each of us strive to cover our bases in taking on a task, large or small, if not exceed its obligations.

Personal excellence is not always rewarded. Nor is excellence always possible. We are affected by issues of wellness, stress, or oversight—all of which are natural, from time to time. But I do believe that at critical moments in life, someone who matters to us will witness our striving for excellence—just as such a person will witness an incomplete effort—and it will make a difference.

But there is a greater ethical dimension to what I propose today.

Much is made of the principle of "service" in our spiritual culture. I do not fully resonate with that concept. I often hear the hollow chime of self-regard when someone claims the mantle of service. But I believe in *effort*, which is the domain of the choice-driven being. To fall short of effort is to be less than fully alive as a striving person. Without effort, one cannot be happy because *one is not truly expressive.*

Effort has the same effect as service, and possibly more. Effort makes you whole—and, within the framework of a given encounter, it makes another whole insofar has he or she can fully experience a result.

Effort fosters trust. Ideally, it builds reciprocity. As with our exercise about respect, however, it must be noted that human relations are marked by inconsistencies. Your delivery of effort or respect will not necessarily be reciprocated.

Yet when a small coterie of men and women willingly acts from principles of effort and respect it marks them as standing apart in life. You will, as part of this self-selected coterie, experience *reciprocity of selfhood*—your reward will be in self-respect and personal satisfaction. This is because you will be living from the arc of self-directed expression and not evasion or reaction.

In *The Varieties of Religious Experience*, William James calls this the feeling of being "consciously right, superior, and happy."

## DAY 22: REJECT COMFORT MEDIA

We are sometimes advised to read things with which we disagree, as though that is a mental stimulant. I question that approach. Given the quality of most expression in the digital era, the things with which we disagree may be of no greater value than those to which we nod our heads.

The point is: most digital media is fleeting, flighty, provocative, repetitive (dates change, themes recirculate), and unnecessary. Our intake is overdone and our time is overburdened.

I believe in a kind of personal fierceness in determining and maintaining a firewall around what media you let in.

Friends press upon you things that you "must" read, view, or experience. But there is, in fact, a silent ledger within you that draws you toward media and expressions that abet private themes you are developing and to which you alone are privy. Honor that.

You owe no justification to another person, peer, or spouse as to the nature of your media diet. Your intake does not require explanations or adjustments, other than to honor the legitimate experience of spending time with another, which may sometimes entail a shared viewing or entertainment that may not top your list but matters to someone in your life. Those are good exceptions.

I am often bombarded with links, articles, and books that people urge me to check out. Sometimes good information reaches me this way, and I am probably behind in my reading in some fields that I care deeply about, such as ESP research and placebo studies. But I go with my passions. As I write this, I am reading a 1966 work of history called *Signal Catastrophe*, about the extermination of the British army in Afghanistan in 1842. I searched hard to find an original copy. My next read is *Finding Joseph I* an oral history of the life of H.R. (Human Rights) the lead singer and songwriter of the punk band Bad Brains. I am currently watching the 1976 BBC dramatization of the reigns of the first emperors of Rome, *I, Claudius*.

Am I missing out on something? Well, probably. I could be more versed in contemporary media. I probably need to dip my toe in further. But time is limited and each of these works, in its way, figures into and augments themes that I am pursuing as a seeker and writer. I simply *want* to be imbibing these things.

What do *you* want to be absorbing? How much are you being taken away from that by peer pressure, conformity, or, as today's exercise suggests, repetitive intake of media (often based in politics or gossip) which serves more as emotional comfort and nest than as an actual source of stimulation and engagement?

Today, and going forward, eschew peer-driven and comfort media. View, read, and experience what you alone want. With apologies to no one.

## DAY 23: PRACTICE SEX TRANSMUTATION

This passage was written on the Vernal Equinox. Our ancient ancestors celebrated this day as one of new beginnings, the dawn of spring, and the renewal of the zodiac. In Persia, Rome, Greece, Egypt, and elsewhere this day has been marked through the ages. May its coinciding with this passage bring promise and renewal to you.

Let me also note that we are on Day 23 of our time together. Twenty-three is venerated as a number of synchronous significance to artists and spiritual thinkers I admire (though do not always agree with) including Robert Anton Wilson, William S. Burroughs, Genesis P-Orridge, Aleister Crowley, and Arthur Koestler.

I did not specifically plan for any of this, but here we are.

Today's chapter is a bit of a departure. I specifically wanted to include a more spiritual—by which I mean extra-physical—element to the book. That is part of my outlook and, if you are reading these words, probably yours, too. At the same time, no "belief" is required.

The important thing is: I want us to have a private method of inner practice to augment the relational and self-developmental aspects of these 30 days. What I love about occultic exercises is the absolute freedom they provide to the individual: to try or not; to experiment; to repeat if useful; to augment or alter.

As I have written elsewhere, I sometimes call my practice anarchic magick. I like to sample and clip and paste and rearrange and try—based on personal election at any given period or moment. Education is also necessary. A musician who cannot play chords cannot play at all. Who cares if you smash your guitar but cannot play it? So, learning, grounding, and know-how matter. The fee earned from all that is, ultimately, freedom. Ability grants you the capacity to "rip it up and start again," as the Orange Juice lyric goes.

So, try what I document in the chapter. See how it goes. As the sun enters Aries, we commence a period of fertility. If the gambit of sex transmutation is right, then that fertility must be broadly defined: it runs through every area of your life, creatively, financially, relationally, and so on. Let this be a day of new expressions or attainments.

# DAY 24: PRESENT RIGHT

Recent this writing, I was listening to an interview with the rap duo Insane Clown Posse. I find them real and brilliant. They were saying that they never appear in public without their makeup. One of them made the point that if an artist is not as instantly recognizable as an action figure, then something is missing.

We are conditioned to believe that ideas about personal presentation are incidental to, if not at odds with, spirituality. But going back to every ancient tradition that has reached us—Egyptian, Native American, Mayan, Hellenic, Zulu, Pacific Islander, and so on—costume, adornment, and body art are a vital part of all ritual and ceremony and are often incorporated into daily life. Symbolism is not expressed through inanimate object alone. It is reflected not only in statuary, bas relief, tapestry, architecture, and painting. Symbol is part of you, too.

Admittedly, such things get commodified, repackaged, and sold back to us. The Clash lamented the phenomena of "turning rebellion into money." The day before writing this passage, I saw an advertising poster in the subway for Google Pay, which depicted a punkish young woman on a skateboard. The image checked every box of independence while reinforcing sameness: the pitch is for uniformity of payment so that your every purchase is tracked and used to predict and manipulate spending. That is the nature of digital commerce and its methods are endlessly intrusive. I have no immediate solution to that other than awareness: that is why a part of this chapter deals with reusing, repurposing, reclaiming, and, when possible, making for self. (There are, of course, greater and more global dimensions to this issue, which may someday involve "data liberty.")

Seen from a certain perspective, Insane Clown Posse is a kind of liberatory movement. Its avid followers, called juggalos, form a network that spreads news about albums, gathers into festivals, follows the band on tour, and so on. Juggalos do their own face painting and make their own merch. As it happens, Insane Clown Posse receives little mainstream publicity. ICP and the juggalos are a fairly self-contained community based on affinity for music, styles, and gatherings, which creates a deeply felt bond. Juggalo style is not wholly dependent on digital commerce, which is notable.

My point is: do everything that you can to create an environment around you, including an *environment of one*, that tells the world, and yourself, who you are. The keepers of spiritual conduct, whether alternative or traditional, sometimes repeat nostrums that make this kind of approach seem off-key or mistaken. Does another know what builds your life? I have found no division between so-called inner and outer. Liberatory gestures in what is considered the outer have tremendous power throughout your being. Give today to that experiment.

## DAY 25: LEAVE THE AIRPORT

I mentioned earlier the statistician's expression: "Life favors action."

Whenever you feel frozen, faced with daunting odds, or dogged by old fears and thus inert in a situation that requires your attention (often my problem when dealing with bureaucracies), it is vital to *act*. One small step can reveal an opening not previously detected.

I am amazed by the number of times that a single phone call, question, request, or decision reveals unseen options.

Now, I must make a confession: Although I have been a fitful student of human nature for years, there are common behaviors that I do not understand. Generally, these behaviors fall under the rubric of avoidance. When people do not have something prepared—such as an assignment, a piece of writing, or a product—they sometimes go silent. I am the opposite. I seek to handle a problem, however imperfectly, as a way of mitigating fear. For some people, or so I gather, fear or stress is mitigated by silence, avoidance, or evading contact. It is not my personal poison, so admittedly I do not understand it. But I can say from experience: action is always better. Even if that action comes in the form of deferral but in actively *explaining* that you are deferring.

I used to tell publicists in the publishing business: "When you do not answer an author's email—that *is* your answer." A non-response says: I don't care. Whatever the backstory, that is the message. I am sure that you have encountered this kind of thing in your own sphere. It is, in my view, the worst possible response. Let us vow never to contend with stress by inertia or unwarranted silence. Such a move always exacerbates, never resolves.

When you are stuck in a bad situation always seek some way to take action. Even if that action involves gathering information on which you may act later. Inner action is still action.

When I was a kid, my father told me, "If a dog chases you and you run, it will bite you worse. If you stand your ground, you may still get bit, but it will be less severe." I do not wish to over-extrapolate from that statement; but I do think it contains a constructive idea. (Of course, if you can get away from the hostility, literally or figuratively, then do so. Not getting bit at all is the best outcome.)

Facing a problem and *acting* almost always results in a better outcome. As with this chapter, many of our exercises can be enacted on a small scale. My mantra: what you do on a micro scale can be repeated on a macro scale. Get the feeling of action today. Step into rather than away from a difficult situation, especially where avoidance is the norm.

## DAY 26: DO YOU ENJOY SUFFERING?

This is one of the most difficult questions to face. It may be the most important in our 30 days together.

Ostensibly, I do not "enjoy" feeling afraid. And yet . . . even though the effects of fear may include pain, the emotion itself—much like anger, aggression, truculence, intimidation, or cries of victimhood—often delivers a kind of thrill. It provides relief from the routines of life. It makes me feel as though I am the center of attention. But it is often negative attention.

If not for a payoff, why else persist in clearly hurtful patterns?

It has been observed that there is a reassuring quality to familiarity, including in painful family dynamics. I have heard the term "trauma bonding." I honor that. But my proposition is based on slightly different premises.

Spiritual teacher Vernon Howard once asked students to write the phrase "false feeling of life" on a slip of paper—and then study it for six months. We crave reward—this "false feeling of life" or thrill—but we often deny the negative manner through which we seek it.

The feeling of a thrill—so evident from gladiatorial events in the ancient world and violent sports media and gaming today (along with much more)—is constantly sought. Watch carefully for whether you gain a sense of contest, aliveness, or thrill, through what is called suffering, either through witnessing, inflicting, or self-inflicting it.

It is rarely easy for me to observe this pattern in my own life. But my contention—and I am working on this with you as I write these words—is that *what is found is generally what is sought*. This is true even when the thing sought reaches us in a form that we complain about. Sometimes complaining *is* the point. Watch today whether your burdens are self-selected as a means to attention, thrill, solicitation of help, relief of boredom, or some other payoff.

I have observed that our biggest adversary is often *overcompensation*. Overcompensation is the means by which we create self-fulfilling prophesies. Fear of rejection, for example, may result in pushing yourself on someone, which inevitably produces rejection. We overcompensate for perceived flaws. And, hence, we bring those flaws, phantom or not, to the fore. It is a strange symmetry. Yet unrealized power dwells within that symmetry, provided we can become aware of it. If events are self-created, then they can be self-altered.

Ask yourself: What am I summoning? Do I really want it? If so, why? If not, why not? And if the event, or the pattern of events, causes me pain, is this summoning a misdirected search for power?

Again: we often get what seek. The arrival may cause suffering but it may also deliver exactly what is sought, albeit with the effect of self-negation. Select positive attention, not negative attention. Select positive expressions of power, not negative ones. Select self-direction versus self-abnegation, especially in relations with others.

## DAY 27: YOU ARE NOT SOMEONE ELSE'S DECISION

I wrote today's chapter because I feel strongly that no solution should be off the table—including ones that our peer groups or cultural nests may not validate.

Orthodoxy does not belong to one side or another. It is a constant of human nature. Hence, one routinely encounters orthodoxies and prejudices within the alternative spiritual scene and its adjacent cultures. Things that are considered "mainstream"—such as money, pharmaceuticals, fashion, affluence, elective/cosmetic surgeries, consumer goods, pop culture, and so on—are sometimes regarded as symptoms versus solutions. But your associations with these things are highly individualized. And solutions can arrive from myriad sources, just as problems do.

I ask you to think really freely about what is right for you. With no one else's approbation. And without feeling bound by handed-down wisdom. Money cannot solve problems? It solves lots of problems. It may not always be available but that should not be conflated with its utility.

Often people who do not possess something hold forth on its limits. Or people who *do* possess something, and would not give it up for the world, talk about the emptiness of prizes, worldly goods, or personal attributes.

The point today is not to favor one outlook or another—but to favor your own.

Even when using metaphysical approaches, in which I strongly believe, solutions may arrive through seemingly established, routine, or ordinary means. So much so that we might brush them aside. For example, who says a solution cannot arrive in the form a pill? Why is that any less miraculous than any other approach?

I encounter people on social media, as I am sure you do, who hold calcified ideas about what constitutes "spirituality." Like any orthodox religionist, they might insist that "true principles" run along certain lines.

People write things like, "The only way to know Truth is . . ." Fill in the blank with their experience. But today we are interested in *your* experience.

In spiritual circles we are sometimes told to verify things for ourselves. That principle must be meant seriously. It cannot mean, in effect, verify something and come back when what you have found matches what I already believe. Today, verify for yourself some solution that may not be supported by your subculture. Determine its value for you alone.

## DAY 28: IS THIS NECESSARY?

The song of necessity is the simplest and most overlooked means of power in your possession.

It is nearly unbelievable how much superfluous behavior we consent to. This is often to alleviate boredom, attract attention, or tell other people what to do (a human passion).

This problem is easiest to see on social media. Try asking before every post: *is this necessary?* For the first time in human history, every random, half-rendered, or immature thought can be announced, memorialized, and forever accessed on digital data bases. It is a disaster. As I write these words, news is circulating of a prominent editor who got fired from a new position for tweets she had made when she was a minor and for which she had already apologized about two years earlier. The risks of frivolity and foolishness online are not to be underestimated. Teach this to your kids.

It took me a long time to learn this lesson. I am still learning it. Social media encourages the dopamine rush of attention and it is addictive. It is so tempting to make a silly, sneering, half-baked, or attention-seeking remark about nearly anything. One hidden debt is that so many exchanges on social media become a contest. A single comment can trigger that contest and enact time-wasting friction. Step out of it.

Likewise, with talking. Watch out for "small talk." You may or may not want to disclose your activities to someone with whom you are thrown in random contact on a commute, dental visit, elevator, or airplane. Most of these encounters actually center on complaining. Watch for that.

A dimension of "find the scissors" is present in this exercise. We often ask people to fetch things for us—"can you bring me the phone charger?"—which we can easily get ourselves without bothering another. This escalates in workplaces where some people seem to dedicate their entire jobs to making work for others. I once estimated that 20% of my workday was given over to correcting simple mistakes or doing things that someone left incomplete. You may calculate a higher percentage in your own experience.

In short, when you abstain from the unnecessary you: 1) reduce possibilities for friction (especially on social media), 2) foster self-sufficiency, 3) avert the resentment of "task dumping" (which is also an ethical violation of another's time), 4) experience the self-respect of carrying your weight, and 5) preserve your attention and energy for tasks that truly matter.

In writing this book, I have been inspired by spiritual teacher Vernon Howard. One night, Vernon told a roomful of students: *"All I'm really trying to say is, why don't you just leave people alone?"* He was exploring how we routinely invade other people's lives and create needless burdens and annoyances. Today's exercise addresses that crisis and, especially in our digital era, suggests a way to stand taller. What you save in time, attention, and energy can be dedicated to more of what truly matters to you. What does matter?

## DAY 29: CHECK YOUR VALUES

Friends, this is our second-to-last day and I saved this chapter for a special place.

If I truly had to boil down this book, if I had to select just those sections that are most certain to enhance your personal nobility—a term we do not flee from—they would be found in the dictum to escape cruel people and the effort to live by the principles in this chapter.

Truth-telling, loyalty, fairness, solidarity—these are ideals that every religious code has sought to capture and has also abused through congregational exclusivity, guild thinking, hypocrisy, and local prejudice. These are, in fact, the values of primeval self-knowledge and we all feel them. They belong to everyone and no one.

As noted, social media is rife with voices that chastise people about whether they have the right kind of spiritual or ethical principles, insights, and associations. By and large, it is blather. Life is conduct. That's it. Expressions of insight mean nothing outside relational conduct.

When someone voices a virtue or insight, my question is: would your boyfriend/girlfriend/spouse/roommate/child attribute such qualities to you? Are you the person upon whom intimates reliably depend? Or would they tell a different story of their experience with you? Would they have different recollections? Be haunted by that before proffering judgments about spirituality, politics, or morals.

As noted earlier, all people consider themselves good, empathic, and unprejudiced. Universally. Hence, what one feels about self is suspect in terms of evaluating honor. I just wrote *honor*—and as explored in this chapter, I reject today's fallow disdain for such concepts.

Honorable behavior includes completing promised work, paying debts and workers, keeping your word, demonstrating solidarity, plain dealing, striving for consistency, abiding by just requests—*and also failing at all these things, and trying again, because they are reciprocity itself; they are, of themselves, the code of human wholeness.*

The smog of human nature is hypocrisy. Hypocrisy often conceals itself behind moral claims of one form or another. The difference between morality and ethics is that the former redounds credit to the speaker and the latter is based in conduct, seen or unseen, appreciated or misunderstood. This is why moral claimants, of whatever nature, are usually hiding something, or they are using the language of virtue to justify force. They disguise this from themselves above all. In George MacDonald Fraser's ribald novel *Flashman* (1969), the antihero says: "I have observed, in the course of a dishonest life, that when a rogue is outlining a treacherous plan, he works harder to convince himself more than to move his hearers."

Today's chapter is not about success but about failure—my own included—to live up to what we *know* are primeval standards of nobility and rightness. You feel them. They are innate. These ideals underscore, and are often sullied by, religion. But never mind legalistic or doctrinal expressions. Embrace primeval values, which I've attempted to trace here, without category. In doing so, you join a chain of seekers throughout history who have sought them with you.

# DAY 30: ONE MISSING THING

I felt melancholy this morning of this writing because it has meant a lot to me to be experiencing these 30 days with you. At the same time, energy must be contained in a vessel or it dissipates. This "miracle month" has been our vessel. There will be others.

My point in today's chapter is not that you must reach the same conclusion about giving that I did—perhaps you will, but perhaps there is a different and equally compelling "missing ingredient" for you.

Philanthropy is important. But my efforts are intended to be personal—starting with how another person is treated, especially in working conditions. It is not a social gesture exactly. Although it can be a social gesture; that is not for me to decide.

The difficulty of solidarity is human corruption. Corruption runs riot. Force seeks expression through any means given it. For that reason, some people do not deserve second chances. Be wary of extending second chances. The overwhelming likelihood is that a second chance will net the same return as the first. And yet we cannot neglect, in the nature of reciprocity and at the risk of personal happiness, treating another with dignity. Life is, ultimately, common.

The world and its political bases are shifting in our generation. It is increasingly difficult to define religious and social positions according to familiar labels. Indeed, even a small degree of friction exposes how little we believe in stated positions or principles.

The spiritual philosopher G.I. Gurdjieff made the haunting observation that the philosophy of most people amounts to: "I like" or "I don't like." There are no other real premises.

Hence, many people who perceive themselves as avatars of free speech would, in an instant, curb free speech that chafes against their wishes. People who extol religious freedom would, in the same instant, erase that freedom for someone whose religion bothers them. People who claim to support democracy would take (and attempt to disguise or perfume) measures to curb or deny voting rights to those they dislike. And so on. It is human nature.

Hence, I not only doubt but reject most enunciations of virtue. What so moved me in the episode of kindness shown to the kids on the beach was the quietness and intimacy of it. One could say that such acts are not a solution to anything. And yet, they predicate everything. Policies arise from (and often corrupt) such principles; but such acts precede policy.

My accountant recently told me that the clients he must chase after for money are often the wealthiest. I do not know why that is but I recognize the behavior. New Thought pioneer James Allen (1864–1912) observed that people tend to be greediest in circumstances of plenty, like birds in a feeding frenzy over a full loaf of bread. I honor Allen's observation but I do not consider it entirely right. People are also brutal and grasping in poor atmospheres, of course. But Allen realized that *plenty does not alleviate avarice.*

Hence, acts of consideration may not alter human nature or individual behavior. Yet I do believe that a small number of people who tend more toward the empathic than spiteful scale of the psyche are capable of modeling ethical behavior. Intimate acts, for good or ill, are remembered because they evoke emotions. An intimate act of solidarity, performed today, may impact another for the rest of his or her life.

Does such an act matter? Does it "come back" to you? If you are drawn to such a self-expression, and I suspect that you are, that is justification enough. It becomes part of the urge to generate, express, and produce. "As above, so below." Express that today.

The intimacy of private generosity reached me as the missing ingredient of my search. It may be yours, too.

May these 30 days and their insights be with you always.

# ABOUT THE AUTHOR

**MITCH HOROWITZ** is a historian of alternative spirituality and one of today's most literate voices of esoterica, mysticism, and the occult.

GABRIEL DEAN ROBERTS

Mitch illuminates outsider history, explains its relevance to contemporary life, and reveals the long-standing quest to bring empowerment and agency to the human condition.

He is widely credited with returning the term "New Age" to respectable use and is among the few occult writers whose work touches the bases of academic scholarship, national journalism, and subculture cred.

Mitch is a writer-in-residence at the New York Public Library, lecturer-in-residence at the Philosophical

Research Society in Los Angeles, and the PEN Award-winning author of books including *Occult America*; *One Simple Idea: How Positive Thinking Reshaped Modern Life*; *The Miracle Club*; *Secrets of Self-Mastery*, and *The Miracle Habits*.

He has discussed alternative spirituality on CBS Sunday Morning, Dateline NBC, Vox/Netflix's Explained, VICE News, and AMC Shudder's Cursed Films, an official selection of SXSW 2020. Mitch is collaborating with director Ronni Thomas (Tribeca Film Festival) on a feature documentary about the occult classic *The Kybalion*, shot on location in Egypt and releasing in 2021.

Mitch has written on everything from the war on witches to the checkered career of professional skeptic James Randi, for *The New York Times*, *Boing Boing*, *The Wall Street Journal*, *The Washington Post*, *Time*, *Politico*, and a wide range of 'zines and scholarly journals. He narrates audio books including *Alcoholics Anonymous* and *Raven: The Untold Story of the Rev. Jim Jones and His People* (the author of which handpicked him as the voice of Jones).

Mitch's book *Awakened Mind* is one of the first works of New Thought translated and published in Arabic.

Mitch received the 2019 Walden Award for Interfaith/Intercultural Understanding. The Chinese government has censored his work.